STRATEGIES FOR UNDERSTANDING AND ENRICHING TODAY'S YOUTH

o o o o o o o o o o o o

Revisiting Our Beliefs and Strategies Pursuant to Socialization Challenges African American Children Face Before and Through Adolescence

Carl Farrell, Jr.

Foreword by Diane McMillan, MSW

STRATEGIES FOR UNDERSTANDING AND ENRICHING TODAY'S
YOUTH

Revisiting Our Beliefs and Strategies Pursuant to Socialization Challenges
African American Children Face Before and Through Adolescence

Published by G Publishing
Detroit, Michigan

Cover design: S.O.S. Graphic Designs, Detroit, Michigan

Printed in the United States of America

ISBN: 0-9727582-7-5

Library of Congress Control Number: 2005925242

DEDICATION

I dedicate this book as a sacred tribute to my Creator and as a special tribute to my beloved three children Steffini, Scott, and Kellie whose socialization yet evolving in adult life I still find exciting.

To my beloved parents, Carl Herman and Mary Elizabeth; to my extended family including mothers of my children and to my adolescent years "rites of passage" mentors I lift your names up "high" and declare this project a tribute to you as well.

AND

To a beloved child Robyn Sampson (Robbie) in memorium who amazed her parents and others with her spirituality and imaginative literary poems and whose intriguing story "The King and His Kingdom" written at age 6, for this author I give tribute.

CONTENTS

ACKNOWLEDGEMENTS

To supporters and friends I say thank you for the thoughtful remarks you extended to me to persevere and for your assurance of personal accessibility to assist during this writing.

I would especially like to note the kindred spirit of these supporters some of whom are co-workers or church family: William Bradley, Marsha Parrish, Regina Washington, Ashara Shepard, Carl Parham, John Frierson, London Sampson, Diane McMillan, Joe Baker, Percynthia Hodges, Yared Tsegaye, Larry Ato Polk and DELgreco Harden.

Moreover, to all well wishers including the outstanding notables in this book whom I've met, via T.V./Radio, book research and/or know personally I say thank you for your cherished wisdom messages.

For her help and encouragement in shaping, the final manuscript, I would like to thank my typist, Cynthia Kelly.

UNIVERSAL VALUES/NEEDS

- The ability to get ones needs met (Spiritual, Mental, Emotional, Physical, Survival)

- The ability to feel/know that one is a success.

- The desire/need to be happy.

- The desire/need to feel important and good at some particular endeavor.

- The desire/need to feel understood/accepted as unique.

- The desire/need to have a feeling of self worth.

- The need to believe in a power greater than ones self.

- The desire/need to have a devoted loving family.

x

FOREWORD

Endowed with much compassion, ability and vision for our youth, the author, Carl Farrell, Jr., has given us an enriching, well written socialization message. He has clearly demonstrated in his literary context the thesis of "Will" and "Faith" and an unrelenting persistence in working with youth. I endorse this project as an essential resource for teachers, counselors, social workers, coaches, youth advocates, parents and other educational leaders to utilize during their curriculum planning, training and/or decision making. I am honored to have conducted Self-Esteem youth workshops with the author as well as having provided lectures on "Winning Strengths" for his students at Project Restore, referred to herein.

Let us dialogue with these book truths which are genuine realities for us to strengthen our resolve with today's youth. "Strategies for Understanding Today's Youth" is truly an opportunity for us, the readers, to revisit our socialization realities as well as adopt those new ones that will help us "champion" our cause. We will meet the challenge!!

– Diane McMillan, MSW
Associate Professor of Social Work – Marygrove College

Strategies for Understanding and Enriching Today's Youth

INTRODUCTION

Guiding and motivating our children to bright futures has been an honorable challenge for most, if not all parents, yet, how have we approached parenting and what about it have we learned to respect? Having posed these questions to myself has led me to focus on the theme, Revisiting Beliefs and Strategies Towards Understanding and Enriching Today's Youth. Commitment to developing healthy positive children takes an earnest loving will, energy flexibility, and an understanding of many ongoing growth changes that often explains their predisposition to make the choices they make or prefer to make. In sharing these beliefs and strategies herein hopefully this literary project will bring pleasant reminders of options, choices and outcomes we have experienced and/or will signal experiences yet to come towards socializing our children holistically.

I have had the opportunity as an African American male born and raised in Newark, New Jersey to reflect on my parents environmental experiences somewhat and their responses to the racial injustices they encountered; i.e., work, wages, housing, health care, leisure/recreation and limitations to opportunities of their choice during my childhood. Notwithstanding, I do recall a treasured childhood with many memorable highlights i.e., eating chicken and dumplings, and that popular bologna sandwich, watching the feats of sports heroes, Jackie Robinson, Don Newcombe and Lenny Moore, church, high school varsity athletics (Football, Basketball and Track), bicycling experiences, church sponsored Boy Scout camping, visits to The Boy's Club and the many pre-adolescent 50 yard sprint races in the neighborhood of Seventh Street and Davenport Ave.

As a Masters in Sociology recipient from Wayne State University in 1973 following matriculation at Tennessee State University (1958-1962) in Health and Physical Education, I have since acquired a heightened interest in socialization and structural practices black families have modeled overtime some of which are cited by E. Franklin Frazier (1894-1962) a black Sociologist. His focus being, not however characteristic of the masses, the Matriarchal Pattern and the Class Patterns in Negro Family Life towards the end of the 19th Century and the beginning of the 20th Century.

As validation Andrew Billingsley, author of the "Black Families in White America" in 1968 gives the names of E. Franklin Frazier, W.E.B. Dubois and Charles S. Johnson as some of the noble social scientist as early as 1930 – 1940 and earlier. He contends they had given deeper interpretations i.e., emerging social class delineations and other theses in explaining Negro Family Life. Moreover, this has helped to dispel subculture inferior characterizations, such as, deteriorating, deviant family life descriptions amongst African Americans who still face racial discrimination and relative unequal access to wealth and comparable life earnings in our society today.

In retrospect the very nature of slavery in the United States with its separation of family groups often resulted in female family heads. A father might be sold and separated from his family, but when the mother was sold, the slave master had to take the children into account, Dr. George Washington Carver's family was reportedly split up. There was disorganization initially following emancipation (1865) but also in time families strengthened and marital unions developed. Reportedly, as indicated in Andrew Hacker's, Two Nations, Black and White, Separate, Hostile and Unequal published in 1992 "families with female heads have increased substantially in the United States with over half in black families"[1] notwithstanding many of these families have survived and prevailed. In family situations where fathers and/or grandparents perform supplemental and or collaborative parenting, relief and added nurturing is realized as in my own parental experience in Detroit, Michigan. I assumed parenting responsibility enthusiastically during my marriage and following a divorce. In keeping with the theme of this project revisiting socialization challenges; families are yet struggling but often prevailing enough to sustain a healthy identity for their children. Not having visited statistics regarding subsistence from fathers not residing in these homes, I trust an appreciable number of children are growing up with collaborative parenting, thus giving more credence to "We will win if we don't quit" (Bishop T.D. Jakes). "This is truth edification for me that we must keep the faith in the socialization of our children while amenable to change. We who are socialization agents seeking truth and success will win. God's word has given us a standard from which to make winning practical decisions if we choose.

Having migrated to Detroit in 1967 following a three year military assignment in the United States Air Force as a 1st Lieutenant Squadron Commander, this author has amassed many career experiences working with adults and for the last thirty years part-time and/or fulltime with youth. He has been a practitioner actively engaged in conducting physical education, providing behavior-modification sessions for client-referred youth in Treatment Programs and providing alternative educational leadership services for a state contracted program. Positions held include YMCA Physical Director and subsequently a volunteer YMCA Basketball Coach (nine years), Part-time Human Resource (Group Dynamics) Instructor/Oakland University, Day Treatment Director/Wayne County juvenile clients, Group Home Coordinator For Boys, Foster Care Social Worker For Lutheran Child and Family Services, GED Alternative School Director/Franklin Wright Settlement and since 1996 a Detroit Board of Education Middle School Physical Education Teacher. In 1993 the Northwestern YMCA awarded Carl Farrell, Jr. a Distinguished Leadership award for Chairing the Strategic Planning Committee pursuant to identifying contemporary facts relative to Education, Health and Physical Wellness, Economics and Social Dynamics that impact the Northwestern Y.M.C.A. and Community.

I have always been connected to socialization practices through study/research and application which has provided this intrinsic interest. It's exciting to revisit socialization beliefs, strategies and blended researched ideas with you.

The age-groupings with whom I have worked in the above occupations including a 14 year period as an Adult Probation Officer (1969-84) have encompassed ages (6-11) but, primarily Pre-adolescence (11-13), Adolescence (13-20) and Adults in the Wayne County Criminal Justice system of Detroit (17 years and up). Again these work experiences and my own children's socialization has peaked my interest to ongoingly highlight healthy socialization strategies. Some of the socialization concepts that develop our children early or as I refer to as antecedent socialization are addressed in this presentation.

This author is impressed with many notable sociologist and psychologist, but the historical references featured herein that impact black families, Dr. James P. Comer of Yale Child Study Center, and Dr. Alvin F. Poussaint of Harvard Medical School who are African American Psychiatrist standout. In their dual authored book "Raising Black Children' they confront the educational, social and emotional issues facing African American children. Pursuant to education they remind us in their question and answer reviews what in the past happened to those youngsters who were denied an education. "In the black world they purport that through sheer determination, black parents have sent their youngsters to school notwithstanding unequal education opportunities; however the educational design was to educate black children to assume menial roles.

Historically, many black boys denied a chance for an education were able to earn a living and support themselves through heavy manual labor-agricultural and industrial. Black women had to accept low-paying, often back breaking domestic work as did my mother. Comer and Poussaint, M. D.'s, reflect that as long as the economy could absorb undereducated people, such youngsters were able to grow and meet their adult responsibilities as heads of households despite the low pay and hard work. But this has been more difficult since the 1960's, when the better paying jobs began to require a higher level of education." [2]

In this written project my position is that the family is a crucial institution of socialization that imparts the earliest teachings and practices before the child progressively interacts with other agents of socialization, schools, community peers, etc. Family agents for socialization during slavery and following Emancipation Proclamation often included a mixture of family members mother, father, grandparents, cousins, uncles, aunts and sometimes trusted acquired family. Towards developing skills, knowledge, attitudes, values, habits, beliefs and cognitive reasoning I have highlighted practices of socialization that can enfranchise our youth through adolescence and prepare them to face the challenges of today and tomorrow.

Of course our youth today are confronted with many challenges, some of which are self esteem issues, strengthening attention spans, academic consistency, peer emotional responses, anger management, conformity, restructured home lives, divorce matters, media imagery, drug use enticement, sexual activity vs. abstinence, family underemployment, etc. The stronger the family pro-action on "You Have Great Potential," "Stay Focused" and "What Do You Want to Accomplish" the better the solution outcome. Can the child our children see themselves happy in the future? As we rejoice in our children's goals, achievements and temporary pauses we give them our confidence to take the next "step."

Before we move into the main text, a noteworthy highlight that epitomizes "We will win if we don't quit" is the life of Frederick Douglass, as the challenge was for him "Who Am I"? and "Who Will I Become?" Certainly we can take a moment to critique briefly his childhood transition to help us examine our hardship past and visualize our children's triumphs yet to come. His original name was Frederick Augustus Washington Bailey, (born February 7, 1818, Tuckahoe, Md., U.S.-d. February 20, 1895, Washington D.C.); a Black American who was one of the most eminent human-rights leaders of the 19th Century. His oratorical and literary brilliance thrust him into the forefront of the U.S. Abolition movement.

Separated as an infant from his slave mother (he never knew his white father), Frederick lived with his grandmother on a Maryland plantation until, at the age of eight, his owner sent him to Baltimore to live as a house servant with the family of Hugh Auld, whose wife defied state law by teaching the boy to read. But Auld declared that learning would make him unfit for slavery, and Frederick was forced to continue his education surreptitiously with the aid of school boys in the street. Upon the death of his master, he was returned to the plantation as a field hand at 16. Later, he was hired out in Baltimore as a ship caulker.

Frederick tried to escape with three others in 1833, but the plot was discovered. Five years later, however, he fled to New York City and then to New Bedford, Mass, where he worked as a laborer for three years, eluding slave hunters by changing his name to Douglass. Mr. Douglass would later become a consultant to President Abraham Lincoln, a District of Columbia Marshall and finally, U.S. Minister and Consul General to Haiti (1889-1891). Mr. Douglass' countenance was special and with a strong constitution to be somebody with a supportive grandmother, he championed many causes. What does his life impact to us? As I reflect in short, it is what we believe is possible that influences our hopes, aspirations, actions and the outcome of plans.

It is hoped that the contents herein will offer helpful strategies and/or support socialization practices already yielding great achievement or signal the success that is yet to come. Again, we will win if we don't quit.

Strategies for Understanding and Enriching Today's Youth

AIM OF SOCIALIZATION

1. Enables children to learn what they need to know about American values in order to be integrated into the society.

2. Enables children to develop their potentialities and form satisfying relationships.

3. Develop self concept.

4. Develop understanding of functional interrelatedness between different sectors and cultures of society.

5. Develop self actualization with appropriate references to significant others and to historical significant others achievement.

6. Teaches social roles.

7. Teaches developmental skills.

8. Develop child self control, independence and appropriate interdependence.

9. Develop adequate appropriate awareness of racism and cultural/racial misrepresentations.

10. Develop concept affirmations about religious worship.

Intentional socialization: Adults impart certain values that they consistently convey explicitly to the child and when they back these up with approval for compliance and consequences for non-compliance this conveyance is referred to as intentional socialization.

Unintentional socialization: The socialization that takes place during human interaction without the deliberate intent of imparting knowledge or values.

Agents of Socialization

- Family
- School
- Peers
- Media
- Community
- Institutions
- Written Word

PREREQUISITE FOR SOCIALIZATION
(Earliest)

Professor Wenar in his text, Personality Development, Infancy to Adult hood, purports that psychologist Yarrow's (1963) research on early maternal care is considered one of the best models of attachment and mothering as follows "(1) Infant needs gratification and tension-reduction (e.g., how quickly and adeptly the mother responds to the infant's expressions of needs). (2) Stimulus learning conditions (e.g., the amount and appropriateness of maternal stimulation of vocal communication and social responsiveness); (3) Affective interchange (e.g... the mother's warmth, sensitivity, and individualization of the infant), and (4) Consistency. The infant characteristics he (Yarrow) studied were intelligence, handling stress, exploratory behavior, social initiative, autonomy and adaptability.

Attachment to the mother is the infant's first significant relation to a human being and it tends to be the prototype for future human relationships. Psychologist also claim that attachment has a practical consequence. It is a prerequisite for most future socialization. The reward of love and the threat of withdrawing love are basic techniques for redirecting the infant from asocial behavior to socially acceptable behavior. Socialization frequently goes against the grain. The growing child does not inherently want to obey so why should the child ever abandon his asocial ways? The answer is that something more compelling is at stake, namely, the pleasure of being loved."[3]

A positive appropriate attachment to parents engagingly through the high-lighted age groupings is essential to our youth's psychological development and socialization. With positive attachment, parents are better able to plan and/or promote better options and choices with their children and/or enable them to come to their own best decision. Important areas, not all inclusive, in which this parental understanding definitely enfranchises our youth are; namely (1) capacity to tolerate frustration, (2) self control, (3) self-trust, (4) self-esteem, (5) concern for others, (6) morality, (7) ideals while other attachments emerge, and (8) responsibility. Self actualization becomes progressively desirable and challenging throughout our youth's development and thereafter.

Age Groups

- o Neonate (New born)
- o Infant (1st yr.)
- o Toddler (1 to 2 ½)
- o Pre School (2 ½ to 6)
- o Middle Child (6 to 11)
- o Pre Adolescence (11 to 13)
- o Adolescence (13 to 20)
- o Young Adult (20 to 22)

ONGOING SOCIALIZATION CONCEPTS/PRACTICES

For this author, there is no doubt as to whether these revisited socialization concepts/practices of parenting among a host of others will yield a treasured harvest. There is a profound esteem that has often come to our intergenerational parents, extended families and others who have had no illusions about paving the way. Our beliefs affect what we expect of ourselves and what we motivate our children and/or reconcile with them to do toward success. We remain mindful of their individuality and uniqueness in the process.

1. While giving loving care continue to seek understanding of the child and encourage him/her to "press on."

2. Continue to give child a trustworthy loving human relationship.

3. Provide personal care.

4. Provide learning stimulation for the child or children i.e., reading, writing, other constructive play, creative number games, checkers, chess, monopoly, DVD games, building toys, communicative music games, arts and crafts, aquarian visits, woodland hikes, competitive athletics, scouting, clubs, "rites of passage" mentoring activities, etc.

5. Family members facilitate and foster a spirit of companionship, sharing and participation to foster positive self esteem.

6. Parents introduce restrictions but always at the level the child can understand thus creating opportunities for better discernment and emotional responses.

7. Child acquires ambition while interfacing with parents to overcome inferiority with strong innate urge to master:

   a) Physical Environment
   b) To seek love
   c) Security
   d) Companionship from adults and peers
   e) Achieve maximum emotional fulfillment and self esteem through achievement and progressive constructive thinking.
   f) To seek information from others such as peers, teacher, or a favored adult; he may read literature or seek part-time work all of which crystallizes his awareness of steps necessary to achieve a distant goal. Meanwhile, school serves as a stabilizing force by structuring the content of what the adolescent will learn and, through grades and promotions, evaluating his performance objectively (powerful).

8. Parent(s) and significant others serve as "rites of passage" models for the child's self efficacy gradually relinquishing family egocentrism.

9. Parent(s) keep abreast of developmental improvements within home environment and community environment.

10. Explicitly point out the effects of the child's behavior on the feelings and well being of others.

11. Recognition by parents that a child's personality is not necessarily the product of parental behavior.

12. Family continues to exhibit loving support and standards of rewards and punishment with regard to discipline but usually within a democratic/authoritative and/or democratic pattern.

13. Child strives to evolve into and as quickly as possible a good student recognizing their strengths and weaknesses and courage to acquire habits that increase academic success.

14. Similarities of child's own behavior and reactions to those of others are stressed and constructive reparations introduced to reduce guilt.

15. Child strives to evolve into a cooperative courageous, socially involved individual with a realistic evaluation of himself or herself.

16. Child works to be on good terms with himself and the community ongoingly.

17. Parent(s) of family show by example good hygiene and cleanliness.

18. Child has to develop firmly established moral principles whose applicability to reality he continually re-evaluates.

19. Family continues to exhibit a praise and prayer life making God an appreciable part of their lives; doing outreach for others edifying and uplifting.

20. Child progresses in examining reality which points out among other lessons that <u>your own personal happiness becomes your own responsibility.</u>

21. Parents are continuously challenged to promote and encourage their offspring to make an increasing number of decisions for him/herself as his/her developing judgment allows.

22. Parents demonstrate consistency in family life with flexibility in handling problems with ongoing improved communication skills which youth will hopefully emulate.

23. Parents provide for physical needs food, clothing, shelter, and health maintenance and safety protection.

24. Parents interpret with child complex aspects of society and monitors child's academic discipline to learn with rewards and consequences as needed.

25. Parents selflessly provide for logistics to have child exposed to athletics, recreation and music; all factors that contribute to self directed ambition.

26. Parents foster and provide understanding of thought provoking "under tones" of racial distortions about African Americans to raise one's level of pride and social consciousness for justice.

27. Parents when the need dictates consults and provides for illegal drug use treatment intervention to restore their child's adaptability in society and for health maintenance.

28. Parents and significant others in the socialization effort promote respect of family core values and discuss traditional societal values, folkways and mores. Such values include honesty, compassion, discipline, industriousness, achievement and success, external community outreach, reverence, governance, devotion to family, forgiveness, courage and gratitude. Discernment skills to increase awareness of racism and discriminatory practices becomes an aim of many African American groups.

29. Parents often plan, promote and carry-out family events or attend and/or participate in events of which the child is a participant to increase bonding to demonstrate love and respect for their child thus "messaging" you are special, don't quit.

30. Parents and significant others towards building the child's identity throughout childhood and reaffirming their accomplishments provide for picture taking thus providing a visual/emotional reminder to the child that she/he is loved and cherished.

31. Parents devote the necessary time for the optimum academic development of their child while building on constructive coalitions with educators and embracing favorable teacher/student attitudinal goals and

higher academics standards, all of which contributes to a successful outcome.

32. Parents with proper empathy know that their children are not "carbon copies" of them.

33. Parents and significant others work with and cultivate the child's multiple intelligences i.e., linguistic, logical-mathematics, spatial, bodily-kinesthetic, musical, interpersonal and intrapersonal, etc.

34. Parents attend to their children as an energetic listener rather than selective listening which is hard work to balance as we have discovered. Communicating and listening out of love rewards the child and parent. Psychiatrist, Dr. M. Scott, Peck, who authored "The Road Less Traveled" book reminds us that, true listening, total concentration on the other, is always a manifestation of love. Dr. Peck brilliantly asserts, to which I intrinsically concur that; (1) "If we give our child/children the same esteem we would give a lecturer; then the child will know him or herself to be valued and therefore will feel valuable. (2) The more children feel valuable, the more they will want to say things of value, (3) That as they often make interrupting utterances of thought we learn that our children indeed have valuable things to say and that they are extraordinary individuals, (4) The more we learn and know about our children the more we will be able to teach. He, Dr. Peck, summarizes that this cyclical process motivates our children to be more trusting and willing to respond to us and afford us the same esteem."[4] In other words, reciprocal love continues to evolve.

Strategies for Understanding and Enriching Today's Youth

FAMILY CORE VALUES (TESTIMONIALS)

**SOCIAL WORK
STUDENT/PARENT 1:**

1) My religious values/faith in God.

2) The ability to accept situations that I have been put in and deal with it in a positive manner.

3) My love for my family.

4) The ability to make an impact in someone's life.

5) One of the most important things that I value is the people that God put in my life to help me through.

6) The ability to see the good in someone no matter what they have been through and encourage them to do better.

7) Evaluate yourself as a parent/and a person and build your self-esteem.

8) Educate yourself about what is in the best interest for your child.

**SOCIAL WORK
STUDENT/PARENT 2:**

Compassion	Nurturing
Love	Fairness
Consistency	Patience
Faithfulness	Encourager
Caring	Good Listener

- -

Around the table talks/ Be a good listener. Spend one-on-one time alone with each child.

A RENOWN MINISTER'S INSIGHT ON PARENTING

- Parents need cooperation; people get tricked believing that good rules are there to trick you (children) rather than preventing chaos. Breakdown in family Rev. Carlyle Fielding Stewart, III asserts is often attributable to moral breakdown.

- Parents need cooperation and honor from their children; avoid maladies by trusting.

- Parents need compassion; children don't be so hard on your parents. Be glad your parents don't let you do what other parents allow.

- Parents need honesty; be honest about who you are or what you are; your answer should be Yes or No. Per Rev Stewart sometimes it's the parents reaction to truth that determines whether the child will bring to you truth.

- Parents need to strive for excellence; nothing surpasses a good attitude. When you give your best you glorify God.

- Student/child the right people will encourage you to seek excellence.

- Student/child don't lower your standards to fit in with mediocre people threatened by your gift.

Adapted from the Reverend Dr. Carlyle Fielding Stewart, III radio ministry 107.5 service at Hope United Methodist Church, Southfield, Michigan.

Strategies for Understanding and Enriching Today's Youth

TWO MODES OF SOCIALIZATION

PARENT/CHILD

Repressive Socialization	Participatory Socialization
Punishing Wrong Behavior	Rewarding Good Behavior
Material Rewards and Punishments	Symbolic Rewards and Punishments
Obedience of Child	Autonomy of Child
Nonverbal Communication	Verbal Communication
Communication as Command	Communication as Interaction
Parent-centered Socialization	Child-centered Socialization
Family as Significant Others	Family as Generalized Other

Source: Adapted from sociology text, 4th edition 1970, Principles of Sociology, Broom and Selznick (adapted readings) Table IV: 2, P 100

❖ Few parents are as consistent as the list implies.

The two preceding Modes of Socialization represent broad patterns of parental practice in America Society found in a Sociology text adapted readings by Broom and Selznick. When we opt to choose one over the other or interchangeably both are we grounded in knowing the extent to which our children exhibit family core values and their unique approval needs? We are also reminded to revisit thinking in principle particularly regarding self-esteem which necessitates approval of self and approval from others. This suggests that we adopt of the two modes more often at least, child-centered interaction. In either mode few parents are as consistent as the list implies.

"In parental participatory socialization the adult assumes responsibility for discerning the child's needs rather than expecting the child to discern the parent's wishes as in repressive socialization." I prefer to use the Socialization Mode Terminology Democratic/Authoritative/Humanitarian suggesting that the parent and child are bonded by love with ongoing validation; that the child knows as well as the parent that he/she through trial, error and successes will mature, that emotional validation should be mutual and reciprocal, that communication must be two-way and honest, that lines of demarcation regarding unsuitable events and places will be addressed and understood and that parental admonishment/discipline of the child is a validation of love.

As the child learns to exemplify family core values and pro-social societal values better, hopefully to an appreciable degree, parental authority is perceived less restraining and/or faultfinding. Progressively more and more self governance emerges age-appropriately particularly during pre-adolescence and adolescence. In this authors described Socialization Mode, reciprocal love and kindness should still manifest between child and parent. This is not a disavowal that uncertainties, alienations, and tensions won't arise with parents but rather the "bonding conscience" will continue to provide a balance to the dilemma of the adolescent i.e., knowing how to respond to the peer group, in other words, knowing in your heart your doing the right thing while recognizing that peer groups can give positive and/or negative support and advise. Moreover, the mutual bond of love established between parents and adolescent helps in the dilemma and provides a better prospect for conflict-resolution and awareness of his/her developmental issues i.e., independence seeking, etc. Better options, choices and out-comes are realized.

Our children will still ask "Who Am I?" and "Who Do I Want To Become?" in self thought and/or with significant others to onwardly maintain hope and fuel dreams.

ADOLESCENT "WHO AM I" WINNING STRENGTHS

Which of these words describe you and/or imagine a close friend describing you as an adolescent? To what degree? Check (√)

	Consistently	Moderately	Seldomly
Communicative			
Busy			
Kind			
Artistic			
Careful/Catches Mistakes			
Convincing			
Friendly			
Loyal			
Distinctive			
Resourceful			
Self-determined			
Grateful			
Planner			
Ambitious			
Individualistic			
Steadfast			
Problem Solver			

	Consistently	Moderately	Seldomly
Strong			
Considerate			
Patient W/Parents			
Interactive/Team Player			
Athletic			
Playful			
Humorous			
Self-Examining			
Respectful			
Goal Directed/Academics			
Encouraging			
Sociable			
Good Listener			
Leadership Skills			
Helpful			
Fair Minded			
Assertive			
Well Informed			
Affectionate			
Moral			
Spiritually Expressive			
Thrifty			
Proper Hygiene			
Parental Bond			
Freedom/Human			
Consciousness			
Community/Up lift			
Volunteerism			
Achiever			
Self Assured			

We are encouraged to continue looking at our children's strengths and developing characteristics to provide opportunities to further develop them.

THE FAMILY

Democracy	Control
Ability to Plan Fearlessness Aggressiveness Exhibition of Cruelty	Obedience Suggestibility Fearfulness Lack of Tenacity
Permissiveness	**Restrictiveness**
Disorderliness Aggressiveness Expressiveness Lack of Inhibition	Obedience Politeness Tendency to Conform
Warmth	**Hostility**

Secure Attachment Competence
Ability to Solve Problems
Ability to Follow Directions
Willingness to Ask Adults for Help
   when needed
High Self-Esteem
Acceptance of Limits on Behavior
Consideration for Others
Internal Moral Standards
	Insecure Attachment
	Rejection of Directions
	Inability to solve Problems
	   without Frustration
	Unwillingness to Ask for Help
	Low Self-Esteem
	External Moral Standards

Two-Dimensional Relationships of Parenting Styles to Children's Behavior

Source: Adapted From Roberta M. Berns, Child, Family, Community, Holt, Rinehart and Winston, Inc. 1974, Pg. 114. Depicts parenting styles to children's behavior, pre school and middle age primarily. Aggressiveness denotes seldom were children of democratic parents the victim of other children's aggression. Societal attention to the democratic style was gaining some and the individual needs of the child as was noted by researchers in 1940's and progressively since.

America Values/Themes (Ethos) Robert Williams, "American Society", 1970

- Achievement and success
- Activity and Work
- Moral Orientation
- Humanitarianism
- Efficiency and practicality
- Progress
- Material Comfort
- Equality
- Freedom
- External Conformity
- Science and Secular Rationality
- Nationalism-patriotism
- Democracy
- Individual personality
- Racism and related group superiority themes

Socialization does not result in complete conformity

Factors encouraging individuality and uniqueness

1) Personal attitudes

2) Biological innate tendencies

3) Temperament

4) Parenting styles

5) Historical reference

6) Cognitive process

Strategies for Understanding and Enriching Today's Youth

COGNITIVE DEVELOPMENT AND REALITY ASSESSING

In preparation for the review of the function of ego, research reveals that Sigmund Freud, a renown 19th/20th Century Psychoanalyst believes that thinking makes behavior more adaptive to reality and serves to check impulsive actions. Often cited and read has been Freud's personality structure Id, Ego, and Super-Ego which is summarized below.

The Id contains drives such as hunger, thirsts and sex functions according to the pleasure principle, that is; it strives to maximize pleasure and minimize pain. Freud's most mature adult personality has been described as containing this infantile core; primitive in content and operation although it may only be observable under stress, such as severe illness or personal tragedy. When we reflect on Ego, the primary task is that of adapting to the environment. By using a special function called reality testing we can distinguish environmental stimuli from wishes and impulses. It requires employing numbers of psychological functions in order to obtain knowledge. Through perception it gathers information about the environment and through memory it stores the information and through judgment/evaluation it compares new information with that stored in memory and thus we can adapt accordingly.

Freud messages with regards to super ego that this ego component contains moral precepts and ideas and whenever the person transgresses the super ego punishes the individual with guilt.

What is the ego operation? It differentiates the objective from the subjective arriving at an accurate understanding of self, of other human beings and of the physical environment. We have unlimited opportunities as humans to draw conclusions from specific events, formulate hypotheses to fit into other memory information systems and ongoingly evaluate our thinking. A mature adult will ongoingly evolve into a more reasonable conscience.

FUNCTIONS OF THE EGO (Self Accuracy)

EGO FUNCTION	ADEQUATE EGO	INADEQUATE EGO
Tolerating Frustration	Can substitute one goal for one that is blocked	Has a Temper Tantrum
Coping with insecurity, anxiety, and fear	Is able to develop psychological "defense mechanisms"	Can only flee or attack
Resisting temptation	Can resist immediate gratification for long-range goals	Seeks promises of immediate gratification
Assessing reality	Adjusts behavior to particular circumstances and people	May see all authority as replicas figures of parents
Facing Guilt	Has guilt feelings and can right a wrong	Has few guilt feelings and tries to evade them
Establishing Inner Controls	Can substitute inner control when external supervision is withdrawn	Quietly falls into disorganized behavior when outside controls are removed
Assessing reality about rules and routines	Does not feel persecuted by rules and routines	Interprets rules and routines as directed against self
Dealing with failure, success and mistakes	Can correct a mistake and is proud of success	A mistake signifies worthlessness; success, absolute worth
Maintaining Ego Integrity	Express, but does not lose, own values in group activity	Gives in easy to the authority of the group

Source: Adapted from Fritz Redland David Wineman, Children Who Hate: The Disorganization and Breakdown of Behavior Controls: The Free Press, 1951, Chapter III, "The Ego That Cannot Perform," pp. 74-140. This is a study of delinquent children with severe psychological and social difficulties.

ERICKSON'S SOCIO-PSYCHOLOGICAL CRISES STAGES TO DEVELOPMENT

The Erickson theory provides us with an integrated construct linking individual needs with the requirements of the culture at each life stage. I understand that as a parent of three, when they were young I wanted a positive outcome for them two girls and a boy in adapting at each human development stage. To understand the Erickson theory one needs to know that each completed prior stage provides for adaptable connectedness to deal with the crises of the next stage (see chart) at which time one is still dealing/learning new coping skills.

Briefly explained, the Erickson Theory, charted as psycho-social stages which impact the self concept begins with infancy the issue of <u>Trust Versus Mistrust</u>. As we recall earlier herein the infant who is sensitively and tenderly cared for experiences a variety of pleasures. "He feels good inside and develops a deep belief in inner and interpersonal goodness. Since his caretaker is reliable, he also develops a trust of others. If he is unloved or erratically cared for he is subject to intense distress, he develops a basic mistrust of others, a feeling that inner impulses and interpersonal intimacy are bad in the since of being sources of pain."[5] In the <u>Toddler</u> stage, Erickson asserts that "the issues of autonomy versus shame and doubt are at stake. It refers to a child standing on his own two feet psychologically and asserting his selfhood at times constructively, and at times arbitrarily and defiantly. Parental handling determines whether he will continue to enjoy his since of autonomy in spite of realistic demands to curb his excesses or whether he will become ashamed of himself."[6]

As we look at Erickson's Initiative versus Guilt crises stage "the child is "on the make" and glories in his powers. Initiative, power and competition become sources of guilt if parents are too intimidating and if their demands are too harsh."[7] The child will internalize their accusing voice in the form of a relentless, accusing conscience thus causing anxiety, perhaps rampant, about initiative and emotional uncertainty about personal decisions.

Finally in middle childhood, there is the crisis of Industry versus Inferiority. The child turns his energies to mastering the world of objects and ideas and to the development of skills. He develops inner standards for a job well done according to psychologist Professor Charles Wenar who discusses in his book Personality Development (Infancy to Adulthood). "The danger here he asserts in reviewing Erickson's position, is that through inadequate or faulty teaching, through prejudice and/or impetuous parental appeasement needs the child fails to develop his ability to master the real world and instead feels inadequate and inferior."[8] I attribute this to parental egocentric insecurities and underestimation/biased constructs of the child's needs thus leaving the child unfulfilled and decreased, a prelude possibly to poorly controlled aggression.

Professor Wenar recognizing theoretical differences among psychologist contends that on most points, however learning theorist and psychoanalyst would agree that the reason for poorly controlled aggression stems from "insufficient gratification of the need for love by cold, rejecting, punitive parents."[9] What answers do we get when we democratic/authoritative/humanitarian parents ask the question "What aggression expressions are developmentally appropriate?" Learning theorist like psychoanalyst emphasize" the role of the parents as models of self-control which favors the control of aggression in the child." I contend we store plenty of what we see our parents do and hear our parents say in our recall memory.

Aggressive pre-adolescent/adolescent behavior can be construed as patterned acts towards others or peers i.e., excessive teasing, group verbal intimidation in school, borrowing without consent, stealing, malicious slander, fighting, etc., with the intent to "bring low" others and/or injure emotionally. Socialization agents have to step-up promptly in these instances with corrective remedies to which the child must adhere including parent intervention as needed.

ERIK ERIKSON (Psychologist)

EIGHT STAGES OF SOCIO-PSYCHOLOGICAL CRISES DEVELOPMENT WHICH IMPACT THE SELF CONCEPT

Infancy: Trust vs Mistrust . . . . 1st year

Toddler: Autonomy vs Shame . . . . Age 2 to 3

Play Age: Initiative vs Guilt . . . . .Age 3 to 5

School Age: Industry vs Inferiority . . . . Age 6 to Puberty (Age 12)

Adolescence: Identity vs Identity diffusion . . . . Puberty to Age 18

Youth Adulthood: Intimacy vs Isolation . . . . .Age 18 to Middle Age

Adulthood: Generativist vs Self Absorption . . . . .Middle to Old Age

Senescence: Integrity vs Despair . . . . Old Age to Death

Erickson characterizes adolescence the next crises stage "as a time when ego identity versus Identity diffusion are, the issues at stake."[10] Fear and mistrust can wipe out an appreciable amount of progress already accomplished by adolescents. Fading in identity, as a result, can disenfranchise them to give up or incite them to reinvigorate their efforts and prevail toward their dreams. Illustratively, the consciousness of faith by chanting or the singing of "We Shall

Overcome" during Civil Rights activism has been a resounding celebration reminder to disavow "ego" ineffectiveness or "ego death" as African Americans, a counter to what Erickson proclaims in describing Identity Diffusion at its worst. For an individual adolescent, being dropped from the football team after a hopeful quest can become a staggering blow to ones identity of having competitive athletic prowess but to "win" the adolescent must reinvigorate with new plans and discernment; not easy without helpful advise. Self mistrust and fear must not prevail or seize the mind consciousness.

In retrospect, of these crises stages we recognize that there is a dynamic interplay of psychological adaptations to new sociological/environmental pressures and biological changes in human development thoughout life. Erickson addresses stage by stage these appropriate ego adaptations as well as pathological results should there be excessive problems like mistrusting one's own ability to hope, in other words turning on oneself. By the time of adolescence, the individual has a unique constellation of aptitudes, interests and values, a unique personality and temperament. How prior crises are resolved determines the adolescent's inner strength and vulnerabilities in the SEARCH for an IDENTITY. Erickson provides a path toward so called normal predictable development bringing about more awareness and maturity.

PERSONAL SELF-ESTEEM ANECDOTES TO COUNTER IDENTITY DIFFUSION EPISODES

As we have discussed Erickson's views on identity diffusion the question that arises is, "Can and how do we restore our confidence should we encounter intermittent diffusion?" I've seen and worked with youth to know their stamina can give way while they reflect and carry out action plans toward their quality of life. Becoming responsible while learning, unlearning and relearning can weigh heavily during the age range about which we speak particularly pre-adolescence and adolescent. A review from a final report of the California Task Force to Promote Self-Esteem, 1991, I remember to be a powerful presentation thus supporting my own beliefs about sustaining and/or restoring identity. I recognize that the year I parented through my children's years of adolescence 1983, 1986, and 2000, were years of great challenges and joy thus contributing to two-way self-esteem. Strategies to which I concur as follows and have used as a parent, can foster a healthier self regard within ourselves. These strategies transcend into answers to the question earlier "Who am I?" and "What will I become?"

1) Accept yourself. Accepting ourselves begins with an honest look at who we are; then I can change accordingly.

2) Trust yourself and others. The psychologist Carl Rogers encouraged people to trust themselves enough to "Feel their own Feelings" and express themselves in their own unique way. We can learn to

evaluate the risks of extending a little more trust, and when warranted, we can take those risks.

3) Set realistic expectations. Our dreams and goals are like orchards; the more energy we put into them, the more they bear fruit. We need goals that are appropriate and attainable. "I want to be an integral part of society and want to grow in my own direction, and I am capable of making competent and responsible progress as I learn."

4) Take risks developing the courage to explore new thoughts, behavior and possibilities; to take appropriate risks; and to venture out across "safe boundaries" is necessary for learning and growth. Change is very frightening, even when it is a change we want. Often we feel more comfortable with a known problem than with taking steps in an unknown direction toward solving it. This is why some of us don't grow.

5) Forgive yourself and others. To forgive means to stop resenting. When we let go of resentment toward ourselves and others, we are able to live constructively in the present. Forgiving releases us from the burden of hostility that eats away at our energy and self esteem. Forgiveness allows us to move on with our lives.

6) You must generate a new consciousness of faith that the best will still happen. Reinvigorate yourself and implement a working plan.

CONTRIBUTORS TO YOUR CHILD'S SELF-ESTEEM

The amount of responsibility we assume is directly related to our self worth, what we accomplish and the amount of respect we experience. Can our children list three people in each category or relationship below who consistently gives recognition for particular accomplishments important to the child? Identify and describe. For the historical persons identify those persons whom you admire; identify their accomplishments and virtues.

Home:

Person	**Accomplishment(s)**
1)	1)
2)	2)
3)	3)

School:

Person	**Accomplishment(s)**
1)	1)
2)	2)
3)	3)

Church: Person	Accomplishment(s)
1)	1)
2)	2)
3)	3)

Contributors

Relatives: Person	Accomplishment(s)
1)	1)
2)	2)
3)	3)

Peers: Person	Accomplishment(s)
1)	1)
2)	2)
3)	3)

Historical: Person	Accomplishment(s)
1)	1)
2)	2)
3)	3)

Our youngsters can be coached to not give up!!

AN ASSET CHECKLIST FOR TEENS AND PARENTS

Teens Parents   How many external assets are present in teen's life?

_____ _____ Parents are loving, easy to talk to and available when teens want
to talk.

_____ _____ Parents frequently take time to talk seriously with their children.

_____ _____ Parents express their own standards for teenage behavior.

_____ _____ Parents talk with their teenager about school and sometimes help
with school work and attend school events.

_____ _____ Parents set rules and enforce the consequences when the rules
are broken.

_____ _____ Parents check on where their teenager is going, with whom and
for how long.

_____ _____ Parents are approachable when the teenager has something
serious to talk about.

_____ _____ The number of nights the teenager may spend out of the home
"for fun and recreating" is limited.

_____ _____ The teenager has frequent serious conversations with an adult
who is not his or her own parent.

_____ _____ The teenager's friends are a constructive influence, are doing
well at school, are staying away from contact with drugs, alcohol
and other at-risk behavior.

_____ _____ The teenager attends church or synagogue at least once a month.

_____ _____ The teenager sees the school atmosphere as caring and
encouraging.

_____ _____ The teenager participates in band, orchestra, or takes lessons on a

Teens   Parents   How many external assets are present in teen's life? (con't)

musical instrument involving three or more hours of practice a week.

_____ _____ The teenager participates in school sports activities or other organizations three or more hours per week.

_____ _____ The teenager participates in non-school-sponsored sports or other organizations three or more hours per week.

Teens   Parents   How many internal assets are present in teen's life?

_____ _____ Tries to do his or her best at school

_____ _____ Hopes to be educated beyond high school

_____ _____ Earns above-average school grades

_____ _____ Does six or more hours of homework weekly

_____ _____ Is good at making friends

_____ _____ Tries to stand up for her or his beliefs

_____ _____ Cares about other's feelings

_____ _____ Is good at planning ahead

_____ _____ Is good at making decisions

_____ _____ Has a positive attitude toward self

_____ _____ Envisions a happy future for her/himself

_____ _____ Shows concern for the poor

_____ _____ Is interested in helping and improving life for others

_____ _____ Holds values that prohibit having sex as a teenager

NATURE OF ADOLESCENCE/HISTORICAL PERSPECTIVE TOWARD EDUCATIONAL ACHIEVEMENT

Adolescent achievement results from many factors of socialization and individual self-determination. The primary issue for the adolescent is to determine his identity; "Who am I?" "What will I become?" Adolescence is an intermediary state between childhood and adulthood usually between 13 years to 20 years. The adolescent wants a sense of community with others. While withdrawing from parents as mediators and their egocentrism they often turn to group peers to find answers, a sense of belonging, friendships and new experiences. Adolescents want rites of passage to adulthood.

Educational achievement is still a primary prerequisite for access to careers and/or increasing one's opportunity for employment and income. The adolescent as he/she rethinks his identity is mindful of his need to make vocational or training choices. Historically for the African American group particularly, persuasive practices to halt any practice toward self achievement was institutionalized. During legal slavery 1619 – 1865 African Americans then referred to as colored, nigra, etc would unrelentingly secure ways of reading books but not without serious risks.

The Declaration of Independence written in 1776 had not recognized the full citizenship of its colored but after the Emancipation Proclamation state government would provide separate provisions for education with many unequal resources. Separate institutions of learning would continue and schools referred to as normal colleges and institutions and schools for secondary instruction would spring-up particularly during and after reconstructtion (See Table Comparative Statistics of Education, Williams, George, History of the Negro Race in America 1619-1880, The Knickerbockers Press, 1882).

COMPARATIVE STATISTICS OF EDUCATION AT THE SOUTH.

Table showing comparative population and enrolment of the White and Colored races in the public schools of the recent slave States, with total annual expenditure for the same in 1879.

States.	White.			Colored.			Total expenditure for both races. a
	School population.	Enrolment.	Percentage of the school population enrolled.	School population.	Enrolment.	Percentage of the school population enrolled.	
Alabama	214,098	106,950	50	162,551	67,635	42	$377,033
Arkansas	b174,253	b39,063	22	b62,348	b13,986	22	205,449
Delaware	31,849	23,830	75	3,800	2,842	75	223,638
Florida	c40,606	bc18,169	45	c42,001	bc18,795	45	c134,880
Georgia	c236,319	147,192	62	c197,125	79,435	40	465,748
Kentucky	d476,870	e208,500	48	d62,973	e19,107	30	e1,130,000
Louisiana	c141,130	44,052	31	c133,276	34,476	26	529,065
Maryland	f213,669	138,029	65	f63,591	27,457	43	1,551,558
Mississippi	156,434	105,957	68	205,936	111,796	54	641,548
Missouri	663,135	428,992	65	39,018	20,790	53	3,069,454
North Carolina	271,348	153,534	57	154,841	85,215	55	337,541
South Carolina	e83,813	58,368	70	e144,315	64,095	44	319,320
Tennessee	388,355	208,858	54	126,288	55,829	44	710,652
Texas	b160,482	c111,048	69	b47,842	c35,896	75	837,913
Virginia	280,849	72,306	26	202,852	35,768	18	570,389
West Virginia	198,844	132,751	67	7,279	3,775	52	709,071
District of Columbia	c26,426	16,085	61	c12,374	9,045	73	368,343
Total	3,758,480	2,013,684	.....	1,668,410	685,942	.....	12,181,602

a In Delaware and Kentucky the school tax collected from Colored citizens is the only State appropriation for the support of Colored schools; in Maryland there is a biennial appropriation by the Legislature; in the District of Columbia one third of the school moneys is set apart for Colored public schools; and in the other States mentioned above the school moneys are divided in proportion to the school population without regard to race.

b Estimated by the Bureau.   c In 1878.

d For whites the school age is 6-20; for Colored, 6-16.   e In 1877.   f Census of 1870.

Strategies for Understanding and Enriching Today's Youth

Statistics of institutions for the instruction of the Colored race for 1879.

Name and class of institution.	Location.	Religious denomination.	Instructors.	Students.
NORMAL SCHOOLS.				
Rust Normal Institute	Huntsville, Ala.	Meth.	3	235
State Normal School for Colored Students	Huntsville, Ala.		2	51
Lincoln Normal University	Marion, Ala.		a5	a225
Emerson Institute	Mobile, Ala.	Cong.	6	240
Alabama Baptist Normal and Theological School	Selma, Ala.	Bapt.	6	250
Normal department of Talladega College	Talladega, Ala.	Cong.	6	93
State Normal School for Colored Students	Pine Bluff, Ark.		4	72
Normal department of Atlanta University	Atlanta, Ga.	Cong.	...	a176
Haven Normal School	Waynesboro', Ga.	Meth.	...	125
Normal department of Berea College	Berea, Ky.	Cong.	(b)	(b)
Normal department of New Orleans University	New Orleans, La.	Meth.		
Normal department of Straight University	New Orleans, La.	Cong.	(b)	91
Peabody Normal School	New Orleans, La.		a2	a35
Baltimore Normal School for Colored Pupils	Baltimore, Md.		4	190
Centenary Biblical Institute	Baltimore, Md.	M. E.	a5	a75
Natchez Seminary	Natchez, Miss.	Bapt.	4	46
Tougaloo University and Normal School	Tougaloo, Miss.	Cong.	6	96
Lincoln Institute	Jefferson, Mo.		6	139
State Normal School for Colored Students	Fayetteville, N. C.		3	93
Bennett Seminary	Greensboro', N. C.	Meth.	3	125
Lumberton Normal School	Lumberton, N. C.		2	51
St. Augustine's Normal School	Raleigh, N. C.	P. E.	4	81
Shaw University	Raleigh, N. C.	Bapt.	5	192
Institute for Colored Youth	Philadelphia, Pa.	Friends.	...	300
Avery Normal Institute	Charleston, S. C.	Cong.	8	322
Normal department of Brainerd Institute	Chester, S. C.	Presb.	3	50
Claflin University, normal department	Orangeburg, S. C.	M. E.	3	167
Fairfield Normal Institute	Winnsboro', S. C.	Presb.	...	390
The Warner Institute	Jonesborough, Tenn.		c4	c149
Knoxville College	Knoxville, Tenn.	Presb.	13	240
Freedman s Normal Institute	Maryville, Tenn.	Friends.	a4	a229
Le Moyne Normal Institute	Memphis, Tenn.	Cong.	a7	a200
Central Tennessee College, normal department	Nashville, Tenn.	M. E.	3	114
Nashville Normal and Theological Institute	Nashville, Tenn.	Bapt.	6	231
Normal department of Fisk University	Nashville, Tenn.	Cong.	5	215
Tillotson Collegiate and Normal Institute	Austin, Tex.		3	158
State Normal School of Texas for Colored Students	Prairie View, Tex.		3	49
Hampton Normal and Agricultural Institute.d	Hampton, Va.	Cong.	e28	e320
St. Stephen's Normal School	Petersburg, Va.	P. E.	8	240
Miner Normal School	Washington, D. C.		5	19
Normal department of Howard University	Washington, D. C.	Non-sect.	2	95
Normal department of Wayland Seminary	Washington, D. C.	Bapt.	(f)	(f)
Total			181	6,171
INSTITUTIONS FOR SECONDARY INSTRUCTION.				
Trinity School	Athens, Ala.	Cong.	2	162
Dadeville Seminary	Dadeville, Ala.	M. E.	...	...
Lowery's Industrial Academy	Huntsville, Ala.		...	...
Swayne School	Montgomery, Ala.	Cong.	6	470
Burrell School	Selma, Ala.	Cong.	5	448
Talladega College	Talladega, Ala.	Cong.	12	212
Walden Seminary	Little Rock, Ark.	M. E.	...	...
Cookman Institute	Jacksonville, Fla.	M. E.	a5	a140
Clark University	Atlanta, Ga.	M. E.	5	167
Storrs School	Atlanta, Ga.	Cong.	5	528

a In 1878.   b Included in university and college reports.   c For two years.

d In addition to the aid given by the American Missionary Association, this institute is aided from the income of Virginia's agricultural college land fund.

e For all departments.   f Reported under schools of theology.

Statistics of institutions for the instruction of the Colored race for 1879.—
Continued.

Name and class of institution.	Location.	Religious denomination.	Instructors.	Students.
INSTITUTIONS FOR SECONDARY INSTRUCTION. —Continued.				
Howard Normal Institute	Cuthbert, Ga.	Cong.	3	66
La Grange Seminary	La Grange, Ga.	M. E.	4	140
Lewis High School	Macon, Ga.	Cong.	2	110
Beach Institute	Savannah, Ga.	Cong.	6	338
St. Augustine's School	Savannah, Ga.	P. E.	...	...
Day School for Colored Children	New Orleans, La.	R. C.	...	80
St. Augustine's School	New Orleans, La.	R. C.	3	60
St. Mary's School for Colored Girls	New Orleans, La.	R. C.	...	60
St. Francis's Academy	Baltimore, Md.	R. C.	...	50
Meridian Academy	Meridian, Miss.	M. E.	...	...
Natchez Seminary	Natchez, Miss.	Bapt.	4	45
Scotia Seminary	Concord, N. C.	Presb.	8	152
St. Augustine's School	New Berne, N. C.	P. E.	...	...
Estey Seminary	Raleigh, N. C.	Bapt.	...	...
Washington School	Raleigh, N. C.	Cong.	3	149
St. Barnabas School	Wilmington, N. C.	P. E.	...	a100
Williston Academy and Normal School	Wilmington, N. C.	Cong.	a6	a126
Albany Enterprise Academy	Albany, Ohio	Non-sect.	4	64
Polytechnic and Industrial Institute	Bluffton, S. C.	Non-sect.	8	265
High School for Colored Pupils	Charleston, S. C.	P. E.	...	...
Wallingford Academy	Charleston, S. C.	Presb.	6	261
Brainerd Institute	Chester, S. C.	Presb.	5	300
Benedict Institute	Columbia, S. C.	Bapt.	4	142
Brewer Normal School	Greenwood, S. C.	Cong.	a1	a58
West Tennessee Preparatory School	Mason, Tenn.	Meth.	2	76
Canfield School	Memphis, Tenn.	P. E.	...	...
West Texas Conference Seminary	Austin, Tex.	M. E.	...	...
Wiley University	Marshall, Tex.	M. E.	a3	a123
Thyne Institute	Chase City. Va.	U. Presb.	3	213
Richmond Institute	Richmond, Va.	Bapt.	3	92
St. Philip's Church School	Richmond, Va.	P. E.	2	100
St. Mary's School	Washington, D. C.	P. E.	...	...
Total			120	5,297
UNIVERSITIES AND COLLEGES.				
Atlanta University	Atlanta, Ga.	Cong.	ab13	a71
Berea College	Berea, Ky.	Cong.	b12	b180
Leland University	New Orleans, La.	Bapt.	a6	ac91
New Orleans University	New Orleans, La.	M. E.	5	92
Straight University	New Orleans. La.	Cong.	b11	d260
Shaw University	Holly Springs, Miss.	M. E.	6	273
Alcorn University	Rodney, Miss.	Non-sect.	10	180
Biddle University	Charlotte, N. C.	Presb.	9	151
Wilberforce University	Wilberforce, Ohio	M. E.	15	b150
Lincoln University	Lincoln University, Pa.	Presb.	a9	a74
Claflin University and College of Agriculture	Orangeburg, S. C.	M. E.	10	165
Central Tennessee College	Nashville. Tenn.	M. E.	13	139
Fisk University	Nashville. Tenn.	Cong.	13	74
Agricultural and Mechanical College	Hempstead, Tex.		...	...
Hampton Normal and Agricultural Institute	Hampton. Va.	Cong.	(e)	(e)
Howard University f	Washington, D. C.	Non-sect.	5	f 33
Total			137	1,932

a In 1878.   *b* For all departments.   *c* These are preparatory.
d Normal students are here reckoned as preparatory.   *e* Reported with normal schools.
f This institution is open to both races, and the figures given are known to include some whites.

Statistics of institutions for the instruction of the Colored race for 1879.—
Continued.

Name and class of institution.	Location.	Religious denomination.	Instructors.	Students.
SCHOOLS OF THEOLOGY.				
Alabama Baptist Normal and Theological School	Selma, Ala. . .	Bapt. . .	1	. . .
Theological department of Talladega College	Talladega, Ala. . .	Cong. .	2	14
Institute for the Education of Colored Ministers	Tuscaloosa, Ala. . .	Presb. .	. . .	. . .
Atlanta Baptist Seminary . . .	Atlanta, Ga. . . .	Bapt. .	3	113
Theological department of Leland University	New Orleans, La. .	Bapt. .	a2	a55
Thomson Biblical Institute (New Orleans University)	New Orleans, La. .	M. E. .	a1	a16
Theological department of Straight University	New Orleans, La. .	Cong. .	1	21
Centenary Biblical Institute . . .	Baltimore, Md. .	Meth. .	a6	a29
Theological department of Shaw Univers'y	Holly Springs, Miss. .	Meth. .	a2	a17
Natchez Seminary . . .	Natchez, Miss. . .	Bapt. .	2	31
Theological department of Biddle University	Charlotte, N. C. .	Presb. .	4	8
Bennett Seminary . . .	Greensboro', N. C. .	Meth. .	2	6
Theological department of Shaw Univers'y	Raleigh, N. C. .	Bapt. .	2	59
Theological Seminary of Wilberforce University	Wilberforce, Ohio .	M. E. .	7	16
Theological department of Lincoln University	Lincoln University, Pa.	Presb. .	a7	a22
Baker Theological Institute (Claflin University)	Orangeburg, S. C. .	Meth. .	2	28
Nashville Normal and Theological Institute	Nashville, Tenn. . .	Bapt. .	6	50
Theological course in Fisk University .	Nashville, Tenn. .	Cong. .	a2	a12
Theological department of Central Tennessee College	Nashville, Tenn. .	M. E. .	4	45
Richmond Institute . . .	Richmond, Va. . .	Bapt. .	10	86
Theological department of Howard University	Washington, D. C. .	Non-sect. .	4	50
Wayland Seminary	Washington, D. C. .	Bapt. .	b9	b84
Total		. . . .	79	762
SCHOOLS OF LAW.				
Law department of Straight University .	New Orleans, La. .	. . . .	a4	a28
Law department of Shaw University .	Holly Springs, Miss. .	. . . .	a1	a6
Law department of Howard University .	Washington, D. C. .	. . . .	3	8
Total		. . . .	8	42
SCHOOLS OF MEDICINE.				
Medical department of New Orleans University	New Orleans, La. .	. . . .	a5	a8
Medical department of Shaw University	Holly Springs, Miss. .	. . . .	a1	a4
Meharry medical department of Central Tennessee College	Nashville, Tenn. .	. . . .	9	22
Medical department of Howard Univers'y	Washington, D. C. .	. . . .	8	65
Total.		. . . .	23	99
SCHOOLS FOR THE DEAF AND DUMB AND THE BLIND.				
Institution for the Colored Blind and Deaf-Mutes . . .	Baltimore, Md. . .	. . . .	1	30
North Carolina Institution for the Deaf and Dumb and the Blind (Colored department)	Raleigh, N. C. . .	. . . .	ab15	a60
Total		. . . .	16	120

a In 1878.   b For all departments.

Summary of statistics of institutions for the instruction of the Colored race for 1879.

States.	Public schools.		Normal schools.			Institutions for secondary instruction.		
	School population.	Enrolment.	Schools.	Teachers.	Pupils.	Schools.	Teachers.	Pupils.
Alabama	162,551	67,635	6	28	1,096	6	25	1,292
Arkansas	62,348	13,986	1	4	72	1	....	....
Delaware	3,800	2,842	....	....	....	....	....	....
Florida	42,001	18,795	....	....	....	1	5	140
Georgia	197,125	79,435	2	....	301	7	25	1,349
Kentucky	62,973	19,107	1	....	....	....	....	....
Louisiana	133,276	34,476	3	2	126	3	3	200
Maryland	63,591	27,457	2	9	265	1	....	50
Mississippi	205,936	111,796	2	10	142	2	4	45
Missouri	39,018	20,790	1	6	139	....	....	....
North Carolina	154,841	85,215	5	17	542	6	17	527
Ohio	....	....	....	....	....	1	4	64
Pennsylvania	....	....	1	....	300	....	....	....
South Carolina	144,315	64,095	4	14	929	6	24	1,026
Tennessee	126,288	55,829	7	42	1,378	2	2	76
Texas	47,842	35,896	2	6	207	2	3	123
Virginia	202,852	35,768	2	36	560	3	8	405
West Virginia	7,279	3,775	....	....	....	....	....	....
District of Columbia	12,374	9,045	3	7	114	1	....	....
Total	1,668,410	685,942	42	181	6,171	42	120	5,297

Summary of statistics of institutions for the instruction of the Colored race for 1879.—Continued.

States.	Universities and colleges.			Schools of theology.			Schools of law.		
	Schools.	Teachers.	Pupils.	Schools.	Teachers.	Pupils.	Schools	Teachers.	Pupils.
Alabama	....	....	....	3	3	14	....	....	....
Georgia	1	13	71	1	3	113	....	....	....
Kentucky	1	12	180	....	....	....	....	....	....
Louisiana	3	22	443	3	4	92	1	4	28
Maryland	....	....	....	1	5	29	....	....	....
Mississippi	2	16	453	2	4	48	1	1	6
North Carolina	1	9	151	3	8	73	....	....	....
Ohio	1	15	150	1	7	16	....	....	....
Pennsylvania	1	9	74	1	7	22	....	....	....
South Carolina	1	10	165	1	2	28	....	....	....
Tennessee	2	26	213	3	12	107	....	....	....
Texas	1	....	....	....	....	....	....	....	....
Virginia	1	....	....	1	10	86	....	....	....
District of Columbia	1	5	33	2	13	134	1	3	8
Total	16	137	1,933	22	79	762	3	8	42

Summary of statistics of institutions for the instruction of the Colored race for 1879.—Continued.

States.	Schools of medicine.			Schools for the deaf and dumb and the blind.		
	Schools.	Teachers.	Pupils.	Schools.	Teachers.	Pupils.
Louisiana	1	5	8	....	....	....
Maryland	....	....	....	1	1	30
Mississippi	1	1	4	....	....	....
North Carolina	....	....	....	1	15	90
Tennessee	1	9	22	....	....	....
District of Columbia	1	8	65	....	....	....
Total	4	23	99	2	16	120

Table showing the number of schools for the Colored race and enrolment in them by institutions without reference to States.

Class of institutions.	Schools.	Enrolment.
Public schools	a14,341	a685,042
Normal schools	42	6,171
Institutions for secondary instruction	42	5,297
Universities and colleges	16	1,933
Schools of theology	22	762
Schools of law	3	42
Schools of medicine	4	99
Schools for the deaf and dumb and the blind	2	120
Total	14,472	700,366

a To these should be added 417 schools, having an enrolment of 20,487 in reporting free States, making total number of Colored public schools 14,758, and total enrolment in them 706,429; this makes the total number of schools, as far as reported, 14,889, and total number of the Colored race under instruction in them 720,853. The Colored public schools of those States in which no separate reports are made, however, are not included; and the Colored pupils in white schools cannot be enumerated.

African Americans were and have been self-determined and history bears witness to Frederick Douglass and many others who learned to read. Books were secured by various methods sometimes from cooperative Whites and/or religious denomination groups. The efforts of free Colored also helped, of which reportedly there had been a 1:8 ratio of free Blacks to declared slaves during the 1780's most of whom if formally educated had been educated in northern schools and; informally in homes during legal slavery. There were as revealed in Lerone Bennett, Jr's. Sixth edition, and scholarly book, Before the Mayflower, approximately 757,000 Black individuals in America at this time.

As we look at the importance of education historically, we are reminded to reflect on the nature of the educational system and the dilemma for blacks particularly in the South even during Reconstruction 1865-1877. The education in the south for blacks was generally inferior to whites. In keeping with the theme "We will win if we don't quit," however, the right to public education and to rise out of slavery was paramount to many blacks. There was Northern philanthropy provisions in addition to legislator provisions; however, an American dilemma a caste system would still exist. In the North, schools were considered less encumbered with segregation challenges and disparities.

However, race prejudice and separate school attendance restrictions often set up by residential demarcation lines did exist, but the educational quality was considered better. It is noted that Southern education for blacks was challenged by the incessant need for families to make-a-living, often sharecropping, un-equal financial allocation practices, and other post-slavery factors. Illustratively, oppressive acts of violence against Blacks to maintain white supremacy parti-cularly and foremost in the south would continue throughout Reconstruction and thereafter, thus hopefully imparting a consciousness of futility amongst Blacks toward freedom and the pursuit of happiness. I say thanks be to God for the likes of Ida B. Wells, a Black anti-lynching activist and notable others, including the American Anti-Slavery Society – founded by William Lloyd Garrison, a white abolitionist. These leaders and others, such as Thaddeus Stevens, Charles Sumner, Sojourner Truth and Henry H. Garnett remained steadfast and courageous in the "We will win Spirit." Meanwhile, many southerners, according to Myrdal, wanted education to train Blacks rather than educate them and a debate would ensue regarding "industrial" versus "classical" education.

For this author, the North and South educational contrast does not translate a meaning that Black "genius" would not emerge appreciably and progressively despite institutionalized funding /attitudinal differences by design. Southern public schools and historical Black Colleges, i.e. Tuskegee, Spellman, Fisk, South Carolina State, Howard, Morehouse, Talladega College, and others, would establish industrious "bench marks" early on for their students whether in industrial skills, teacher training and/or wider liberal options yet to emerge. Marion Wright Edelman, presently a voice for children and families as founder of the National Children's Defense Fund, has a southern education background. She was born and raised in Bennettsville, South Carolina and graduated from Spellman College in Atlanta and Yale Law School. She was the first Black woman to pass the bar in Mississippi. Likewise, Mary McLeod Bethune, who was born earlier in Maysville, South Carolina in 1875, benefited from a southern education. She studied at the Scotia Seminary in North Carolina and became a civil rights spokesperson for which she received awards as did Ms. Edelman. Ms. Bethune founded the Bethune Cookman College of Daytona Beach, Florida.

Moreover, Dr. Benjamin Elijah Mays, born on August 1, 1894 to tenant farmers and former slaves would embrace his earliest education, likewise, in South Carolina. After college in the north with a Ph.D., he would become President of Morehouse College in 1940 following a Dean position at Howard University in 1935. Mays was a "light of wisdom" for many students at Morehouse, one of whom was an undergraduate in the mid 1940s and became an outstanding civil rights crusader, Dr. Martin Luther King.

Unquestionable, the legacy of Benjamin Banneker also distinguishes the "We will win spirit" with particularly his steady evening persistence in watching and studying the stars. He would become an astronomer and mathematician and is the earliest born of the preceding pioneers, born in the 1700's. His schooling, author Lerone Bennett, Jr. asserts, was in an area around Baltimore, Maryland. He would become known for his first almanac in 1792. Formidably, with explicit words of candor he would announce in a letter to Thomas Jefferson his detestation of slavery, according to Bennett.

We have just reviewed briefly the dreams and unrelenting diligence of four accomplished notables all of whom were educated during their formative years in the south. I am most grateful for their legacy of "Will" and "Faith" along with multitudes of parents, extended kinship and mentors, past and present, who have "Fought the good fight" while reminding our youth "You are Somebody," and to "press on."

Let us now look at the consciousness of a people with an equalitarian vision as we look at the forthcoming chart that compares school attendance percentage by race, ages 5-20. This author of Strategies Toward Understanding and Enriching Today's Youth discerns a substantial improvement difference in attendance by Negroes compared to Whites beginning in 1870. This attests to rapid adaptation with provision improvements and looking to a future comparable to those with first class educational opportunities.

ATTENDANCE IN THE UNITED STATES, AGES 5 – 20, BY RACE: 1850 – 1940

Year	Number	Negroes Percent of Population Aged 5 – 20	Whites Percent of Population Aged 5 – 20
1850	24,461	1.7	52.9
1860	32,629	1.8	56.0
1870	180,372	9.2	51.2
1880	856,014	32.5	58.2
1890	999,324	32.0	55.4
1900	1,083,516	31.0	53.6
1910	1,644,759	44.7	61.3
1920	2,030,269	53.5	65.7
1930	2,477,311	60.0	71.5
1940	2,698,901	64.4	71.6

Source: Adapted from Gunnar Myrdal, "An American Dilemma", The Negro. Problem and Modern Democracy, Volume II: Harper Torch books, Harper and Row Publishers, New York, page 42. Considered one of the best political commentaries on American life ever written the American Sociological Review contends. Figures calculated from 1850 – 1890 from E. George Payne's "Negroes in the Public Elementary School of the North," Annuls of American Academic of Political and Soc. Science, 1928 pg. 224. Figures for 1900 to 1940 from collaborative U.S. Bureau of Census, Payne's calculations and others.

The legal access to public school equal education would become law in the Brown vs the Board of Educational (Kansas) Supreme Court Decision in 1954, won by NAACP attorney, Thurgood Marshall and team. Black community leaders and political organizations, i.e. the National Association For the Advancement of Colored People (NAACP) would continue to litigate and crusade for relevant educational changes while harkening to the hearts and souls of African Americans to be steadfast and watchful for "benign neglect."

Notwithstanding the great and notable achievements of African Americans, North, East, South and West, there is still a sizeable underclass many of whom are yet striving towards success. There is a number of at-risk minority youth and youth at large for whom specific designed programs need to be instituted for remediation in reading comprehension, mathematics, science, language arts, computer skills training and career counseling which will save America's white and black in the midst of crises in preparation for adulthood. The adolescent, the primary age group focus of this book, is mindful of his/her deficits and/or skill levels in academics which will impact their choices and adaptation during their identity crisis period.

NOBLE ADOLESCENT EDUCATIONAL ACHIEVEMENT

Student's who rebound from crises decline, have always been amongst us throughout African American Communities. Emphasis on core values i.e. responsibility integrity, honor, perseverance, passion and compassion aggregately brought forth along with strategies to meet special needs of adolescents through special programs has been beneficial for decades. Head Start an early Pre-School Program has catapulted our youth to high achievement. Our socialization aims including raising educational achievement even during separate and unequal education and/or defacto segregation with the intent to handicap blacks has brought forth the "We Shall Overcome" spirit.

Twentieth Century schooling in urban centers where predominately African Americans have resided in the 1980's and 1990's has seen much upheaval in the politics and tax based issues and lingering exploitive practices where black children attend schools. Fortunately a group of visionaries brought an idea to the forefront recognizing that many children who had strong determination needed intervention to insure their careers and adult success; otherwise would they have become dropouts permanently?

Let us review this vision and the accomplishments of a "dynamic" program launched in Detroit, Michigan by an outstanding Task Force prompted by a Historical African American run Social Service agency, Franklin Wright Settlement, Gerald K. Smith, Director. The Final Narrative/Statistical Report of Project Restore in present tense follows with information categorized; (1) Introduction, (2) Instructional strategies, (3) GED Profile, (4) Testing/Enrollment, (5) Curriculum and motivation including attendance, (6) Career Plans and (7) Summary and student testimonials. This author Carl Farrell, Jr., joined

Project Restore as Assistant Director in June 1988 and subsequently became Director. I contend it was the team work effort by an awesome staff and student ambition that accomplished this noble educational mission before its closing.

Unfortunately the attendance count shortfalls of (22) students short of 50% in January 1991, (12) students short of 60% in July 1991 and (15) students short of 60% in September 1991, represented a loss of money allocations from the State in the amount of $60,160. This would result in a decision to close Project Restore in December 1991, as the student attendance trend had become irreversible and unless the State rescinded the attendance criterion as it was before 1991 expenses could not be met by Franklin Wright Settlement. Nevertheless, we were successful for an appreciable period as you will discover.

INTRODUCTION

An American Crisis, the failure of large numbers of urban city youth to graduate from high school prompted Franklin Wright Settlement Inc. in 1986, to assume leadership in setting-up an Alternative Education Program. With the cooperation of a Community Advisory Task Force Project RESTORE was created and began operating in July 1987, and remains open to accommodate daytime and evening students. Targeted for at-risk students who minimally read at the sixth grade level and with a capacity to accommodate (75) students daily we've continued an aggressive program at 481 W. Columbia in Detroit. The program has managed to keep its doors open despite the bleak prospect of losing funding but, our appeal to the good conscience of the community leaders is based on the measurable success of the program. In presenting this report of goals and outcomes we will cover the fifteen month period July 1990 through September 1991. Our students, mostly African American males, come to us for holistic services social/motivational support, career guidance, employability skills training and particularly academic skill preparation to qualify for a GED Diploma. For this reporting period our enrolled students have come from various referral resources.

The Department of Social Services our paramount funder usually sends referrals more heavily during recruitment in July and August before the fall semester in September. Referral sources whom we've usually accommodated and enrolled their clients since the inception of the program are high school officials, human service agencies for at-risk males and legal officials. Walk-ins from single parent homes of low income and some students who walk-in from households of two parents have been serviced at RESTORE. Most of our students who are from single parent homes average seventeen to eighteen years of age and they have reasons for their difficulty in traditional school settings. Our survey results show in order of impact factors causing dropping out to be;

(1) expulsions and suspensions, (2) absenteeism, (3) communication breakdown with family and school, (4) problems with teachers/poor self concept and (5) school disinterest and peer pressure including gang conflict. Problems at home created many difficulties for the students.

Notwithstanding, our program design for at-risk students at RESTORE has rendered significant measurable success. Crucial in delivering our services has been the commitment of a problem solving staff comprised of a Vocational Counselor (laid off), Job Developer (laid off), Social Workers (3) (two positions unfilled), Curriculum Specialist, Assistant Director (position unfilled), Director, Secretary/Receptionist (2 positions but, 1 unfilled), Maintenance/driver part-time, Accountant and Teacher Staff of two full-time and eight part-time. Positions now unfilled had been filled before July 1991 enabling the full complement of staff to carry-out holistic services, including, but not limited to the following:

- Student Recruitment
- Formal Counseling
- Team Intervention
- Employability Skills/Computer Skills Instruction
- Job Search Activities
- Organizing Field Trips
- Coordinating Efforts For Guest Motivational Speakers
- Special Attendance Award Programs for Student Retention
- Team Teaching
- Predictor Skill Testing Often Enough To Identify Students Ready For GED Testing
- Collaborative Efforts with Agencies For information Sharing and Volunteer Assistance Whenever Possible.
- Teachers Sharing Strategies For Effective Teaching All of Whom Usually
- Teach at Least (3) of the (5) Core Subjects, Specifically, Science. Math, Writing Skills, Social Studies, Language Arts/Reading Comprehension.
- Daily Group Motivational Sessions conducted By All Support Staff on a Rotational Basis.
- Coordinating Family Night and Open House Activities.
- Maintenance of Attendance Visuals for Each Enrolled Student.

Ongoingly performances of students are measured against attendance goals, tabe testing, skill performance in class, predictor test scores and teacher recommendations, the outcome of which, is grade improvement or movement from Lab 7.9 or below to Pre GED or 8.0 to 9.9 to GED or 10.0 to 12.0 grade equivalent to a GED Diploma.

I.   INSTRUCTIONAL STRATEGIES:

The test of General Educational Development GED was revised in 1988, to evaluate the candidates' cognitive development according to Bloom's Taxonomy which measures students understanding of information, application, analysis, synthesis ability and ability to make judgments about the validity of the information. The ability to teach these skills requires consistent teacher motivation, explanation with learning style discernment, demonstration, student participation and observational evaluations to measure their students' progress toward an objective(s). Teachers who have taught at Project RESTORE fit the following profile:

- Flexible in their teaching style and methods.
- Ability to act as a change agent with students.
- Effective classroom management skills and plenty energy resources.
- Sincere interest in both their students and subject matter.
- Ability to build skill confidence in students to master new material.
- Positive attitude toward the goals of Project RESTORE and the holistic concept.

Our teachers on staff have undergraduate and graduate degrees and/or graduate level education courses, previous experience with at-risk student populations backgrounds in psychology and training in classroom behavior modification backgrounds, in special education, department head experience and have research interests such as educational psychology, test and measurement and curriculum development. Also a strong study skills resource person exists on staff.

Project RESTORE has made every attempt to encourage the development of creative and effective teaching practices through regular in-house meetings, seminars, and group curriculum development projects. Within the constraints imposed by budget and limited physical space, Project RESTORE has provided our students with many alternative learning activities. Some of the most successful and frequently used methods include:

- Audio visual presentations.
- Guest speakers and lectures.
- Field trips.
- Hands-on science studies and projects.
- Computerized instruction.
- Group learning activities within the classroom.
- Peer tutoring.
- Educational games.
- Team teaching.
- Drama and talent showcasing activities.
- Public speaking opportunities.
- Essay and poetry writing.
- Independent and group computer projects.
- Student selection of plays for reading and interpretation to develop critical thinking skills.
- Relative ethnocentric cultural content.

The teacher work-force of (ten) for day and evening classes at RESTORE allows delivery of instruction of each subject simultaneously at the three levels, Lab, Pre GED and GED to meet student skill levels which varies with each student. Students are able to go to the level to which he/she is recommended anytime during our open enrollment semesters. New students come into classes throughout the semester after diagnostic testing which identifies their skill level Lab 7.9 or below, Pre GED 8.0 to 9.9 or GED 10.0 to 12.0 grade level equivalency for each core subject.

II.   PROFILE OF OUR GED GRADUATES FOR PERIOD JULY 1990 THROUGH SEPTEMBER 1991

The ultimate aim of the students is to acquire the GED Diploma. This credential is recognized as a key for further education and/or employment. Proceeding often with a passive learning style initially, students who succeed must make a transition to a more assertive learning style. Review of student learning styles necessitates flexible teaching modalities. Below is highlighted each student graduate's passing score compared to the minimum passing score of 225 in the State of Michigan. Below also are facts to illustrate academic deficits that were overcome and the necessary length of enrollment time at Project RESTORE to qualify for a diploma.

Simulated testing conditions before going to a testing site off premise builds student confidence. However, students experience the usual nervousness at the Ruthruff Examination Center and yet 90% of the time pass on the first try. The highest official GED score for a student in our program since its opening in 1987 is (324) illustrated in the GED Profile section. The female student who earned this score increased her reading and mathematical grade level by (2) years over a (9) month enrollment period during which time she was sixteen (16) years of age and had to wait until age 17 to qualify for testing:

II. RESTORE GRADUATES PROFILES (D.S.S. denotes Department of Social Services). (Table used for Entry Scores)

Graduate Name	D.S.S. Eligible	School Entry Date	Last H.S. Grade Completed	Grade Equivalent Entry Score	Duration of Enrollment	Age	Mon./Yr. Program Completion	Official GED Score
Tyjuan	No	5/90	11th	9.2	4 months	19	9/90	231
Vincent	No	6/90	9th	9.2	3months	18	9/90	235
Robert	No	2/90	10th	10.0	7 months	18	9/90	228
Michael	No	8/90			1 month		9/90	234
Rochelle	No	4/90	10th	8.9	5 months	18	9/90	225
Dion	No	10/90	10th	7.6	11 months	17	9/90	230
Leland	No	12/89	9th	8.0	11 months	18	10/90	228
Lillian	No	9/90	9th	9.6	1 month	18	10/90	247
Dorian	No	1/90	9th	7.8	11 months	17	11/90	225
Charles	No	7/90	11th	8.3	5 months	17	11/90	225
Brad	Yes	7/90	11th	8.3	4 months	18	11/90	225
Michael	Yes	3/90	9th	7.8	7 months	18	11/90	253
Roderick	No	5/90	10th	6.3	7 months	18	12/90	250

II.   RESTORE GRADUATES PROFILES (D.S.S. denotes Department of Social Services).

Graduate Name	D.S.S. Eligible	School Entry Date	Last H.S. Grade Completed	Grade Equivalent Entry Score	Duration of Enrollment	Age	Mon./Yr. Program Completion	Official GED Score
Burnette	Yes	10/89	9th	7.8	1yr/2 months	18	12/90	225
Natasha	No	9/90	9th	10.0	3 months	17	12/90	225
Marquis	Yes	5/89	9th	10.0	3 months	17	12/90	230
Cass	Yes	12/89			1 year	17	12/90	225
Ralph	Yes	9/90			3 months	17	12/90	225
Chandra	Yes	9/90	9th	8.6	3 months 2nd admittance	20	12/90	225
Ayanna	No	11/90	9th	9.5	3 months	17	2/91	231
Sylvester	Yes	9/89	9th	9.9	1 yr/6 months	18	2/91	225
Michael	Yes	11/91	9th	7.0	5 months	21	3/91	236
Antoine	Yes	9/90			6 months	20	3/91	227
Sanquanetta	Yes	9/90	9th	8.7	7 months	17	3/91	232
John	No	1/90	10th	8.7	3 months	17	3/91	261
David	No	2/91	10th	10.0	2 months	17	3/91	225

Name	D.S.S. Eligible	School Entry Date	Last H.S. Grade Completed	Grade Equivalent Entry Score	Duration Of Enrollment	Age	Mon./Yr. Program Completion	Official GED Score
Lamon	No	11/91	10th	8.8	5 months	17	3/91	225
DeMark	Yes	3/91	9th	10.0	3 months	19	6/91	227
Roman	No	10/90	9th	7.8	9 months	17	6/91	237
Frank	No	1/91	11th	10.0	6 months	18	6/91	242
Orlando	Yes	4/91	10th	8.2	3 months	17	6/91	225
Cynthia	Yes	1/91	10th	8.2	6 months	17	6/91	230
Arlana	No	4/91	11th	10.0	3 months	18	7/91	225
Marlin	No	2/91			6 months	18	7/91	231
Dana	No	1/91	9th	10.0	9 months	17	9/91	*324
Robert	Yes	1/91	11th	7.8	9 months	21	9/91	248
Rico	No	4/91	10th	10.9	5 months	18	9/91	233
Sam	Yes	5/91	8th	10.4	4 months	18	9/91	225
Stephen	Yes	3/91			7 months		10/91	225

Strategies for Understanding and Enriching Today's Youth

Continue: GED PROFILE

A review of GED graduates grade equivalent increases in reading comprehension and mathematical computation while enrolled at RESTORE, using the Table Measurement Test, resulted in an average of 1.5 to 2.0 years improvement. Moreover, the average completion time for students who tested at 12.9 in either math or reading comprehension upon entry into the program was 5.7 months.

III.   TESTING AND ENROLLMENT

Our program has, despite contractual language which stipulated eligible clients as Department of social service clients only, admitted non-DSS candidates deemed suitable to compensate for DSS client referral shortfalls and partially poor client test performance (reading comprehension below 6th grade). This policy of admitting suitable high school dropouts not on Public Assistance, had always provided us with a respectable enrollment usually close or beyond the (75) number to be served. Servicing non-DSS candidates continued until May 1991, after which we couldn't due to unavailable Skillman monies. A Job Start Program making referrals to us from DSS had been, since September 1990, an enhancement to Project RESTORE'S program inasmuch as it increased the number of applicants for testing. We averaged an enrollment of six Job Start clients per month while the other (81) students we averaged were usually ADC dependents, other agency public assistance clients (i.e., Star of Commonwealth), public school expelled student walk-ins, Food Stamp or Medicaid recipients.

TESTING and ENROLLMENT

Month/Year		Number Testing	Number Passed	Percentage Passed	New Monthly Enrollment
July	1990	29	17	59%	5
August	1990	56	42	75%	25
September	1990	47	39	83%	25
October	1990	22	16	73%	11
November	1990	20	14	70%	9
December	1990	23	19	83%	6
January	1991	35	23	66%	10
February	1991	33	22	67%	16
March	1991	48	32	67%	14
April	1991	31	22	71%	25
May	1991	29	17	59%	9
June	1991	15	9	60%	9
*July	1991				9
August	1991	18	14	78%	0
September	1991	27	19	71%	26

Candidates who pass must show commitment during admission conferences conducted by Social Workers and are usually accompanied by a support person, however, if they don't show up for the conference and/or orientation the third and last admissions step they're not counted as an enrollment. This Testing/Enrollment process allows us to contract with the student and the student likewise can determine their commitment to a (6) six month to (12) month accountability of regular school attendance. We believe those who don't show or who even finish the three step process which usually takes (1) week and don't attend classes have unresolved problems or have doubts. Of those candidates who passed (158), during January 1991through September 1991, as indicated above, we enrolled (118) or 75% which means 25% never enrolled or reported for class instruction. For the entire (15) month period we averaged a 70% test passing rate (6th grade reading level or better).

*The (9) new students in July 1991 were either re-admitted students and/or carry-over students from prior months who decided to follow through. July was the beginning of summer vacation and the program was prohibited from taking Non- D.S.S. applicants that accounts for the downslide plus rumors of the program closing.

IV.   CURRICULUM, ATTENDANCE AND MOTIVATION

Our attendance goal for all students was targeted at 80% but our contract called for 50% attendance for January 1991 and 60% respectively for April, July and September 1991, to qualify for unit funding of $1,360 per student in fall, winter and spring and $820 for summer. Unfortunately we've had shortfalls of our monthly budgeted unit numbers of (65) and summer (43) with this new contract mandate, which was our first year implementing same; designated dates were established for attendance headcounts to be taken in January 1991, April 8-19 and September 16-27. The outcome for January was as follows:

Goal	Actual	Percent of Goal	Shortfall	Percent of Enrollees
65	43	66%	22	53%

*January Figure (43) included (3) 60% to 80% and (8) and better.

Students making 60% and better attendance for other head count months follows:

Month	Goal	Actual	Percent of Goals	Shortfall	Percent of Enrollees
April 1991	65	62	95%	3	68%
July 1991	43	31	72%	12	41%
September 1991	65	50	77%	15	62%

We used cash stipend awards and special visiting guest speakers as incentive. It was a monumental task getting (62) students in April and (50) students in September qualified for the $1,360 per each student from state funding. The social work staff conducted an average of (208) monthly phone calls and (33) monthly group motivational sessions for the period January 1991 through September 1991. This is a difficult population to keep focused and notwithstanding our efforts, a monthly average of (14) students or 16% dropped out of the program. The average monthly enrollment was (87) for the period July 1990 through September 1991.

Motivation

Based on motivational unit contract language beginning in January 1991, no less than (3) contacts per student per month, one each in a group session, individual one-to-one counseling and collateral support we attained appreciable success. As staff decreased, however, units depreciated somewhat from the goal which was usually (81) units, meaning (81) students receiving (3) contacts per month. In excess of (81) units no revenue dollars were authorized.

Month and Year		Total Enrolled	Unit Goal	Unit Actual	Percent Success
January	1991	123	81	89	109%
February	1991	97	81	85	105%
March	1991	94	81	95	117%
April	1991	91	81	80	99%
May	1991	81	81	71	88%
June	1991	78	81	67	83%
July	1991	73	81	65	80%
August	1991	64	81	50	62%
September	1991	81	81	61	75%

V.   CAREER PLANS OF GED GRADUATES

Career planning is an integral part of the program ongoingly and students frequently change goals. The Vocational Counselor before her lay-off in July 1991 had compiled career planning information and held formal counseling sessions. The absence of desired follow-up information of the GED graduates to determine their ultimate placement has to date not been tracked given the lay-off of our staff persons and students transient nature. However, we applaud the students who have applied for school and special training with the help of a volunteer Ms. Gayle Thompson of Marygrove College. Her Financial Aid counseling and other advice has proven beneficial since August 1991.

CAREER PLANS OF GED GRADUATES

Name	G.E.D. Age	Career Goal	Training Plan	Applied Yes	No
September (90)					
Tyjuan	19	Navy	Comm. College	X	
Vicent	18	Army	Wayne State	X	
Robert	18	Engineer	Wayne State	X	
Ronald	18	College	*Employed	Unk	
Michael	N/A				
Dion	17	Marines	Comm. College		X
Rochelle	18	Beauty School	Virginia Farrell	Unk	
October (90)					
Lillian	18	Nursing	Wayne State	X	
Leland	18	Mechanic	Fast Track/Mach	X	
November (90)					
Michael	18	N/A	Comm. College	Deceased	
Dorian	17	Computers	College	Unk	
Brad	18	Unk	Unk	Unk	
Charles	17	Unk	Unk	Unk	
December (90)					
Burnette	18	Accounting	Wayne State	X	
Rodney	18	Criminal Justice	Wayne State	X	
Ralph	17	Computers	Wayne State	X	
Natasha	17	Cosmetology	Votech		
Chandra	20	Unk	Unk	Unk	
Marquise	17	Art School	Wayne State	X	
Castere	17	Undecided	Wayne State	X	
February (91)					
Ayanna	17	Nursing	College	X	
Sylester	18	Construction	Voc. Tech.	X	
Michael	21	Undecided	Voc. Tech.	Unk	
John	17	Bus. Management	Comm. College	Unk	

Name	G.E.D. Age	Career Goal	Training Plan	Applied Yes	No
Sanquanetta	17	Undecided	Wayne State	X	
Lamont	17	Unk	Unk	X	
David	17	Pre-Med	Wayne State	X	
Antione	20	Undecided	Wayne State	X	
June (91)					
Cynthia	17	Social Worker	College	X	
Orlando	17	Bus. Admin.	College	X	
Roman	17	Service	1 yr. College	X	
Frank	18	Marines	2 yrs. College	X	
Demark	19	Bus/ Admin.	Det.College of Bus.	X	
July (91)					
Marlin	17	Chef	*Employed Wayne State	X	
Arlana		Computer	Wayne State	X	
September (91)					
Dana	17	Bus. Admin	*Employed Wayne State	X	
Robert	21	Writer	*Employed College	Unk	
Rico	18	Bus. Management	College	X	
Samuel	18	Employed Bus. Management	College	X	

*Currently Employed

VI. SUMMARY AND TESTIMONIALS

We express our gratitude for this challenge and the funding which we hope will continue. A tremendous labor intensive effort has culminated into a sound holistic educational system for at risk students at Project RESTORE. Support staff and academic staff have rendered invaluable services. These service performances by staff not heretofore mentioned are very worthy of acknowledging now:

- Placement test sessions.
- Semester end conferences.
- Student academic reviews.
- Progress reporting to parents.
- Post tabe testing.
- Career training sessions.
- Occupational assessments.
- Admission conferences.
- Special conferences.
- Family night.
- Recruitment drives.
- Group and individual employability sessions.
- Coordinating efforts for ID.
- Lunchroom duty.
- Commendable staff and faculty attendance.

Recommendations

1. Greater funding support with a realistic competitive salary base.
2. Full staff implementation.
3. Admission of a wider array of students in need.
4. Cash summer school stipend provisions to encourage summer enrollment in a (12) month run school.
5. Provisions for performance goals successfully met by staff to earn bonus revenue.
6. An extended contractual term.

Strategies for Understanding and Enriching Today's Youth

OUR STUDENTS' TESTIMONIALS 1, 2, 3

STUDENT 1 TESTIMONIAL

In 1987, when FRANKLIN WRIGHT SETTLEMENT was enrolling its first student I was at Beaubien Middle Student. I was getting average grades but, I wasn't ready to establish good relations with authority figures. I felt like they were against me. I was narrow-minded and had a need for individuality.

I moved on to Southfield Lathrop in 1989 and there I learned a lot about other cultures. However, I felt that this school wasn't suited for me. I then enrolled at Mumford High School in March 1990 in the 11th grade where I was doing the best that I could do but, problems arose with authority figures. Later that year at Mumford I was experiencing difficulty with a particular teacher in American History who seemed to be challenging me constantly and the "Old Me" retaliated which resulted in a termination. Mumford authorities claimed that I was insubordinate. Detroit Public Schools area D officials gave me the choice of going to Cooley or Northwestern. My GPA was 2.0 at this time.

My Uncle Leon knew of Project RESTORE and my entire family supported me. My mother, father and friends have been great sources of motivation for the "New Me."

Project RESTORE'S mission I was not totally aware of, or, the acceptance I would receive, so, when I enrolled in January 1991 I had mixed feelings. Around April 1991/I started realizing that the teacher, counselor, motivation speakers, the Director and other staff members were very concerned and gradually I didn't feel alienated, or hostile toward authority, and my outlook changed. I am proud to say that after (10) months I'll be taking my GED test Tuesday, November 12, 1991 and moving on toward getting my degree n musical engineering.

STUDENT 2 TESTIMONIAL

"When I started attending Project RESTORE, I could care less about school. I had low self esteem and an overall low self image. I was 16 years old and I thought I had no foreseeable future. Out of 3 years of traditional public high school and 5 different schools, I was going nowhere fast. I was in the 9th grade 3 years straight."

"By the grace of God, I finally realize my true potential. I felt good about my self, I wanted to learn, and I made my previously disappointed family proud of me."

"Fortunately, I have an extremely supportive family, but for a long time that wasn't enough to give me the incentive to do better. I had to do it for myself; Project RESTORE helped me to become a more responsible person. Since all students go through an interviewing process, the staff is able to determine what people really <u>want</u> to attend. And all students come on a voluntary basis; no truant officers visiting students' homes, no preaching counselors and administrators, no babysitting. All progress is completely up to the student's ambition."

"At the present time, I am attending school for manicuring, I have good paying job, and I plan on attending Wayne State University next fall."

"I recommend Project RESTORE to anyone who's ready to better themselves and anyone who has the ability to succeed but is in dire need of a place where people actually care!!!"

STUDENT 3 TESTIMONIAL

I'm 19 years of age. I dropped out of High School in 1989 at the age of 17 and was attending Cooley High School. I dropped out, because I was only in the 10th grade and I didn't want to be in the 12th at the age of 19th. My parent had neglected sending me to school and I had to go to a Foster Home for a while. Then I heard about Project RESTORE. My worker called and made an appointment; from there I started classes on October 1, 1990.

The adjustment I had to make was to attend school everyday and stay focused, so I could obtain my G.E.D. The staff gave me confidence and showed me how to achieve my goals.

I completed my G.E.D., November 14, 1991; further more, I'm going to Henry Ford Community College in January to take classes in Accounting and Business Administration.

ADOLESCENT HYPOTHESES

Hypothesis 1:

A healthy unrelenting, socialization process will produce a normal functioning adolescent who will acquire an appreciable regard for Educational Achievement with minimal school performance problems.

Hypothesis 2:

The adolescent peer group and continued but less egocentric family support system continues to provide balance to the dilemma of the adolescent and these variables will increase his acceptance of self and others particularly among the ones with whom he has similar interests and mutual respect.

Strategies for Understanding and Enriching Today's Youth

RISK FACTORS THAT THREATEN AND/OR DIMINISH EDUCATIONAL ACHIEVEMENT

1. Acquired attitudes of low achievement

2. Disorganized family Life

3. Excessive Punitive Parenting Style

4. Drugs/Substance Abuse

5. Low economics and low parental expectations

6. School System apathy/restricted teaching methodologies

7. Suspension track record/poor peer interpersonal relations

8. High unemployment and decreasing economic opportunities

9. Contraculture behavior

10. Behavioral Disorders

11. Teenage Pregnancy

12. Involvement in criminal justice system

13. Poor study habits

14. Job discrimination

15. Gang activities/Violence

16. Child abuse/neglect victimization

17. Funding disparities/Funding delays

18. Superiority myths and stereotypes

19. Negative Political Attitudes

20. Racial Discrimination

CONDITIONS/FACTORS THAT ENCOURAGE EDUCATIONAL ACHIEVEMENT

1. Early Achievement and ongoing meaningful social interaction

2. Drive for competence/rewards throughout socialization period

3. Reading comprehension abilities

4. Consistent nurturance

5. Motivation/Mediation learning/Holistic Approach

6. Peer Acceptance from reference group in which education is valued

7. Family members and significant others whose attitudes reflect approval and re-enforce primary caretakers commitment to rewarding children

8. Self Affirmation

9. Cognitive process a challenge

10. Absence of prolonged dysfunctional factors in family unit

11. Historical references for achievement success impetus

12. Community apprenticeships and net working/involvement

13. School/Corporate Partnership

14. Extra-Curricular-Activities

15. Minimal Developmental Emotional delays

16. Early Career Planning

17. Youth Advocacy

18. Attendance Incentives

19. High quality community and school leadership

20. Ongoing self actualization

21. High Expectations

ADOLESCENT AGE APPROPRIATE COGNITIVE DEVELOPMENT

1. Draws conclusions from specific events and able to formulate hypotheses to fit into other general systems; observation provide opportunities for deductive reasoning

2. Creates Philosophy of Life

3. Creates theory of aesthetics

4. Wants to explain universe

5. Can reflect on the quality of his thinking

6. Dual feelings still exist, however, with self aggrandizement and selfless devotion to others.

7. Discovers he can't impose his answers on the world

8. He must work cooperatively with adults

9. Reflection is not to re-order experience but to predict and interpret it

10. Can evaluate his own thinking

Strategies for Understanding and Enriching Today's Youth

GENERAL CHARACTERISTICS DESCRIPTIONS IDENTIFIED WITH TRANSESCENT YOUTH
(Not a Full Pledged Adolescent)
Age 10 TO 14

Every child is different, however, psychologist are still given us new perceptions of adolescence and one such stage still encompassed in the crises focus is the transescent stage coined by Donald Eichhorn in which youth differ from full pledged adolescents which this author will address following some personal insights acquired from students of his Middle School.

As reviewed in what was highlighted earlier about identity/identity diffusion you had to be thinking about what trials, issues, fears, responses, aims etc concern African American Youth.

In this age range I have seen a variety of behavioral types in the middle school setting; namely the extrovert adaptive with infrequent negative conflict, or anger venting episodes, the adaptive usually bent on getting early approval and amenable to leadership assignments, the self aggrandizement type seeking feedback too often, by negative attention seeking behavior to foster his/her popularity and/or to nurture his/her clique and those who appear somewhat introverted to some degree and may delay joining in with peers or isolate themselves. Notwithstanding, I have witnessed appreciable periods of consistent affective satisfaction and educational growth in these students often enough to know they want to achieve and do achieve. In other words it's discernable by commission or omission behaviorally that they are acting as pre-adolescents/adolescents all of whom want their needs met while still learning and gaining social acceptance. While learning many academic subjects these students I see as a Physical Education teacher are challenged to achieve. Teamwork and competitiveness is encouraged and other broader aspects. We review the lives of sports heroes and their life challenges to make an imprint that something that might seem impossible is really a challenge to have you prepare and dare to fulfill your dream of becoming Whom You Are To Become. For instance a review of Wilma Rudolph's life, a great Olympian runner in the 1960's who was challenged with polio and was not supposed to walk can spark an I Can Do Something very meaningful in my life. Also through the medium of Physical Education our children get a chance to perform fitness test, assess the outcome and discuss benefits from gym and swim i.e.; improve self-esteem and confidence, improve long term weight control, learn the purpose of heart output readings via pulse readings and learn to identify muscle groups impacted by various exercises. Discussions about these benefits and the physical skill achievements in multiple activities helps bring out their identity while improving their self worth thus minimizing fears and fear responses.

Have you parent, teachers, and/or caretaker asked your child and/or youth lately, What Do You Want To Become As An Adult? The results are interesting and having engaged youth for these answers raises their consciousness that more sooner than later he or she needs to pursue a plan to become good at something useful by society. The following are some of the ambitions one of my classes revealed that would fulfill them:

Random Middle School Sample 7th/8th Grade Student Responses To What Do You Want To Become As An Adult?

- Singer
- Pediatrician
- Veterinarian
- Teacher or Doctor
- Teacher or Doctor
- Optomologist/Tennis Player
- Pediatrician Architect
- Judge/Lawyer
- Psychologist
- F.B.I. Agent
- Nurse

Dancer/Teacher
Lawyer
Basketball Player
Football Player/F.B.I. Agent
F.B.I. Agent
Doctor/F.B.I.
Court Worker
Football Player
Artist
Football Player
A Hooper/Basketball Player

If these choices are intrinsic and believable to each of these students "What planning is necessary" and when shall it begin? "Why would it be attainable?" and "What support and/or role models have you begun to seek for answers and/or reading sources?" What motivation do you have to achieve your dream? "What kind of options, choices and outcomes have you experienced in the past that suggests you would accomplish a future goal of this magnitude? "We are going back to the Nature of Adolescence "Who Am I?" and "What will I Become?" As this probe manifests, our youth particularly before or during adolescence will attract and/or seek peers and adult significant others with whom to probe, explore and discern. Remember, parents may become the quintessential motivator or are probably already the primary significant other motivator in instilling ambition. How do we, parents, relate to this? How do we also relate to them seeking independence? Does the empowerment assist our children to discover? How do we know we are raising self reliant, responsible children? Do we seek advice and assistance ourselves? What positive reinforcement reflections do we exchange with our children to help shape their identity? As we reflect on the transescent that follows I ask "Are we learning how to teach our children how to evaluate themselves better in preparation for age 15-20?" Again Donald Eichhorn and other child-growth research authors such as, Paul George and Gordon Lawrence, in their book,

Handbook for Middle School Teachers (1982), have addressed the unique developmental characteristics often identified with ten-to-fourteen year olds. I acknowledge as others do that Dr. Donald H. Eichhorn coined the phrase transescence ages (10-14) which led to a newer embrace of the Middle School concept. He amassed substantive research in psychology, sociology, education and as an education administrator and scholar. The following reviews key highlights from researchers of this distinctive period of transition thus giving keener awareness of transescent needs. This distinctive period has been cross referenced typically as pre-adolescence.

CHARACTERISTICS OF THE EMERGING ADOLESCENT (TRANSESCENCE)

1. During these years ages of 10 to 14, youths are beginning to be aware of imminent body changes, and they seem to be characterized by restlessness and the need to be physically active. These students may exhibit:

   a. Increased interest in the physical aspects of the body, including its functions and changes.

   b. Generally rapid, though irregular, physical development with resultant differences among peers due to uneven growth and development.

   c. Awkward and uncoordinated movements due to bone growth not coinciding with muscle growth.

   d. Considerable attention to personal appearance and concern with irregularities, such as skin blemishes, scars, obesity, etc.

2. There seems to be a desire on the part of youths of this age to begin to assert their need for independence –especially their independence from adults. In a sense, by breaking away from adults, they are asserting their own individuality. These students often:

a. Have ambivalent desires: want <u>freedom</u>, but fear the loss of certain <u>securities</u>.

b. Become more independent, yet still feel the need for direction and regulation.

c. Attempt to identify with adults other than parents.

3. While transescent youth are in the process of beginning to establish Some degree of independence and <u>individuality</u>, they tend to begin to establish a stronger sense of a group identity with their age peers. Hence, they begin to display the well-known adolescent phenomenon of increased group <u>conformity</u>. These students tend to:

a. Conform with "in" styles, such as clothing and hair style.

b. Desire to be "different," yet within the overall limits of peer conformity.

c. Adhere to peer group standards along with awareness of "acceptable behavior" within the peer group.

d. Show considerable <u>peer consciousness</u>: strong need for a feeling of belonging to a group.

4. During this transescent years, youths begin to experience an increasing <u>sexual awareness</u>, so that girls begin to be more conscious of their characteristics and needs as females, and boys begin to be more conscious of their characteristics and needs as males. These students exhibit:

a. A more advanced physical maturity on the part of girls than of boys at the same chronological age.

b. In the early part of the transescent period, there is a tendency to prefer one's sex. This is more marked in boys than girls.

c. In later stages boys' and girls' interests in the opposite sex tend to become more openly manifested to selective admissions of being sexually active to peers or trusted others.

5. Youths at this age begin to expand their horizons, and there is an increase in diverse interests. Their worlds are tending to expand beyond the neighborhood to include greater varieties of people with a diversity of life styles. These students are beginning to:

   a. Have a concern for "right," "wrong," and social justice.

   b. Have a concern for less fortunate "other."

   c. Seek approval of and acceptance by adults.

   d. Show interest in races and cultures other than their own.

   e. Desire opportunities to exercise selectivity in the choice of food, activities, and friends—with frequent changes in "close" friendships.

6. Youths during the transescent years begin to put the skills they have acquired in the elementary schools to use in a variety of situations. Thus, where children at the elementary level tend to concentrate on acquiring the skills themselves, transescent youths begin to use the skills they have acquired —not only in the school itself, but in their lives generally. These students may experience:

   a. A desire to make their own evaluation of suggestions from others.

   b. An interest in making fuller utilization of basic skills used in elementary school.

   c. Strong, intense interests, not always sustained, in various pursuits.

7. In the process of using various skills in a greater number of areas, transescent youths begin to see various relationships that exist between these areas. These students seem to:

    a. Be interested in both concrete and abstract exercises and be more able to deal with abstract concepts than formerly.

    b. Desire opportunities to express originality on an individual basis.

    c. Desire opportunities to participate in practical problem-solving situations.

8. As youths begin to approach adolescence, they become more and more aware of the social phenomenon of adolescence. They have heard a good deal about "being a teenager" and about all the folkways and mores of the teenage culture. As they approach these years, they begin to feel apprehensive about how they will fit into this teenage world. In this sense, then the transescent years are characterized by a good deal of apprehensiveness about the impending adolescent years. These students appear to:

    a. Evaluate personal capabilities, both attributes and limitations.

    b. Be sensitive to criticism of personal short comings and often easily offended.

    c. Need experience with frequent success and desire attention and recognition for personal efforts and achievements.

    d. Be anxious, doubtful, and confused about their physical and intellectual development, social relationships, and adult authority.

9. Transescent youths begin to develop a <u>distinct self-concept</u>. Striving to understand their changing selves, they seek activities to help them psychologically procure their individual maturation. Transescents tend:

   a. To begin to understand that they have certain limitations and certain strengths and while they may not be as capable in particular areas as some other students, they may be more capable in other areas.

   b. To ask the question, "Why am I different from other students my age?" or conversely, "How am I like other people my age?"

10. "Transescents" seem to be more "<u>dichotomized</u>" than any previous generation, and they sometimes run to extremes. Thus, transescents may:

    a. Exhibit a wide range of overt behaviors and moods, thus being alternately quiet-loud, shy-boisterous, fearful-confident, anxious-assured, and so on.

    b. Tend to split into two groups such as the "ins" and the "outs." Additionally, transescents often seek and/or are sought to align with established or beginning "in" groups which "messages" to them a common identity, or identity about which the transescent is curious for developing a sense of belonging. Some members of peer groups can become delinquent but usually these groups with some expected inconsistencies exhibit a wide range of adaptive norm behaviors having (learned acceptable behaviors for given situations).

    c. Some transescents are more self directed than other directed and depending on family influence may have the inclination to conform to institutional norms sooner.

As we look at mental developmental processes in transescents authors George and Lawrence target on the question, what are the main cognitive development processes of transescents? This has to do with primarily six themes of development they assert; including:

"1. From concrete into abstract thinking;

2. From an egocentric (my point of view is the only one) into sociocentric (learning other points of view)

3. From a limited into a broad perspective of time and space (judging sizes and shapes and having future perspectives)

3. From a simplistic into a complex view of human motivation (judging reasons for behavior which is not consistently in the thinking of transescent)

5. From reliance on slogans towards the construction of a personal ideology; and

6. Development of a capacity for forming concepts that stretches from lower order into complex, higher order conceptualizing"[11]

Socialization agents parents, teachers and significant others are instrumental in recognizing biological changes and the child developmental nurturing needs along developmental paths.

Peer group members can be used as socialization agents by adults with positive incentives to induce desired behavior from others to foster a common goal/or norm behavior.

DESIRABLE MIDDLE SCHOOL EDUCATOR TRAITS
(Preferred for Transescents)
Ages 10 – 14

Essential but far from exhaustive the following traits are listed in nonpreferential order by Donald H. Eichhorn in his 1966, published book the Middle School:

"**Personal Security:** The insecurity of transescents requires daily examples of adults who exhibit confidence and faith in themselves.

Understanding: As the emancipation process develops, teachers may be of help to youth by being good listeners and by showing an interest in students.

Resourceful: It has been suggested at length that experiences are crucial at this age group. A teacher must not only be aware of this need but also should cognitively react in a divergent manner in providing the diversity of needed experiences.

Adaptability: Being flexible is a plus being able to continually alter one's daily schedule is a necessary quality for middle school teachers.

Enthusiasm: Transescents profit from an enthusiastic adult. Teachers who are cynics will tend to stifle rather than motivate curiosity necessary for learning experiences.

Cooperative: In the educational model stress was placed on interrelatedness of curricular content and flexible scheduling. These points will require considerable faculty interaction.

Sense of Humor: Teachers who fail to see the humorous aspects in daily human involvements may find difficulty in relating to transescents.

Ongoing with the thought process of traits, Eichhorn espoused that the educational model for transescents calls for administrators with exceptional instructional leadership and sincere personal interest in students beyond just organizational ability.[12]

A FINAL WORD

WITH

PRACTICAL APPROACHES

TO

UNCOVER ADOLESCENT

ISSUES AND STRUGGLES

A FINAL WORD

Looking at socialization concepts and practices allows us to become more enlightened and fosters us to re-evaluate our actions as socialization agents. We have many wonderful parents well informed and willing to remain steadfast and flexible in imparting skills, morality, belief systems all of which become subject to the evolving youth who needs unrelenting socialization. Parents may opt to render a democratic authoritative/humanistic parenting style properly and or perhaps participative to insure ongoing meaningful parent/child social interaction.

Psychiatrist Comer and Poussaint in addressing parents in Raising Black Children convey a message that "we need to provide our children with a strong sense of belonging and communicate in a way that's suitable for your child's age thus making it more possible for the child to discern and respect the message intended by the parent."

Remember that the stage of adolescence per Erickson's, Comer's and Poussaint's and Wenar's message is often regarded as a time of adaptations with the challenge of learning, re-evaluating and relearning, about "Who Am I?" "What Will I Become?" and "What Is My Action Plan To Move My Life Forward?" as I interface with family and "significant other" socialization agents. The African American adolescent and other ethnic adolescents are faced with a physiological revolution and multiple challenges including the coined "transescent stage" characteristics, all of which contribute to shaping his/her identity depending upon their responses to them successfully or otherwise. Of course the African American child, in my opinion must acquire knowledge about their African heritage which better prepares him/her for identity issues, and moreover, gives discernment/insight about inequality, discrimination and historical liberation strategies.

In summary I say, find out emerging adolescent, as early as possible what has been declared your purpose through partnership with your parents, significant others and your God given insight. As declared in messages from three great pastors Bishop T.D. Jakes, Rev. Carlyle Fielding Stewart, III and Rev. Wendell Anthony that reign in my heart and memory are "We will win if we don't quit" (Bishop Jakes), and "Excel as God would have you excel" (Rev. Stewart). "Seize the opportunity in the lifetime of the opportunity," my church home spiritual leader, Rev. Wendell Anthony of Fellowship Chapel, declares and a second noted quote he asserts is, "History is a guide post to the future not just a lamp post for the past." These anointed stewards of the Word remind me that God wants consistency in our "walk" with Him.

I offer the following discernment guidelines; Middle School Adolescents struggles, Adolescent Awareness Issues, Self and Other Directed Progress, Typical Teacher Observations of students, 2004 Student Responses, Ten Action Signals that Ignite Action Plans, What Do I Value In Life Questions and Obstacles to Success Cause Us To Stretch.

To today's youth, while recognizing the influence of peers during your adolescence, do you have a desire to listen to advice on becoming a young adult, meaning committed to doing your best to exercise your best judgment during your development? We parents and significant others believe in your success and your ongoing transformations while viewing you as a special individual destined for a great purpose. I offer the following:

In Middle Schools Adolescents Struggle With To Varying Degrees All or Some of the Following Behaviors

(Indicate whether you have had or presently have these STRUGGLES)

Never, Rarely, Often or Sometimes?

		-N-	-R-	-O-	-S-
Yes	**No**				

1. Blaming others for trouble you're in.

2. Aggressiveness toward peers/aggravations.

3. Self monitoring of Do's and Don'ts as well as rule violations.

4. Knowing when to seek immediate gratification or defer gratification depending upon the situation.

5. Adapting to conformity in general i.e., noise tone in school, improving student/teacher communication, etc.

6. Improving peer relationships and finding possible common interest.

7. Improving study habits to excel academically.

8. Minimizing anger and understanding cause and effect.

9. Fleeing or verbally attacking when things don't go your way and refusing to acknowledge being pre-warned.

10. Recognition from your peers about achievements you've accomplished.

11. Engaging in mental tasks with energy and enthusiasm to acquaint one self with and to comprehend new material and its connection with prior lessons.

Strategies for Understanding and Enriching Today's Youth

Awareness Issues for Adolescents

1. Confronting issues that our youth must often address and need helpful assistance to progress with better understanding through developmental stages are below.

   (a) To what extent do you think about the issues below either daily, weekly or otherwise in an effort to get a sense of understanding about your self? Mark either Rarely, Never, Often or Sometimes. If you think about the Issues daily write in "D" under often other wise use check marks under any appropriate column.

   (b) Which are the top six issues listed from which you have been experiencing the greatest amount of stress and anxiety?

Awareness Issues	Awareness Issues
• Giving Proper Behavioral Responses	Recreation
• Understanding Peer Attitudes	Anger
• Understanding Adult Views	Competitiveness
• Dress Appearance	Honesty
• Nuisance Behavior to Others	Reliability
• Promoting Goodwill	Quality/Doing a task well
• Threats of Violence to Adolescents	Behavioral Effect on Others
• Freedom to Function/Fewer rules	Comparing Yourself to Adults
• Intimidating Others	Comparing Yourself to Peers
• High Ideals	Making Money
• Acceptance From Females/Males	Future Career
• Sexual Involvement	Peer Acceptance
• School Achievement	Avoiding Trouble in School
• Approval from Parents	Fighting with Peers
• Love/Closeness to Others	Creating Problems
	Embarrassing to Parents
• Pressure to Use Drugs	
• Health Issues	Setting Goals for Future
• Committing A Criminal Offense	Immediate Vs Deferred Gratification

ADOLESCENT SELF - AWARENESS SURVEY

To what extent do you think about the issues listed below either <u>daily</u>, <u>weekly</u> or <u>otherwise</u> in an effort to get a sense of understanding about yourself? If daily, write in "D" below the often column. Ask youth if they have any questions regarding these issues before completing the Self-Awareness Survey. Check ( ) appropriate column.

A. AWARENESS ISSUES	Rarely	Never	Often	Sometimes
1. Giving Proper Behavioral Responses	_____	_____	_____	_____
2. Understanding Peers Views or Attitudes	_____	_____	_____	_____
3. Understanding Adult Views or Attitudes	_____	_____	_____	_____
4. Dress Appearance	_____	_____	_____	_____
5. Nuisance Behavior To Others	_____	_____	_____	_____
6. Promoting Goodwill	_____	_____	_____	_____
7. Threats of Violence To You By Others	_____	_____	_____	_____
8. Freedom To Function With Fewer Rules	_____	_____	_____	_____
9. Intimidating Others "Discing"	_____	_____	_____	_____
10. High Ideals	_____	_____	_____	_____

Strategies for Understanding and Enriching Today's Youth

	Rarely	Never	Often	Sometimes
11. Acceptance From Females or Males (circle gender)	_____	_____	_____	_____
12. Sexual Involvement	_____	_____	_____	_____
13. School Achievement	_____	_____	_____	_____
14. Approval From Parents	_____	_____	_____	_____
15. Love/Closeness to Others	_____	_____	_____	_____
16. Recreation	_____	_____	_____	_____
17. Anger	_____	_____	_____	_____
18. Competitiveness	_____	_____	_____	_____
19. Honesty	_____	_____	_____	_____
20. Reliability	_____	_____	_____	_____
21. Quality/Doing A Task Well	_____	_____	_____	_____
22. Your Behavioral Effect on Others	_____	_____	_____	_____
23. Comparing Yourself To Adults	_____	_____	_____	_____
24. Comparing Yourself To Peers	_____	_____	_____	_____
25. Making Money	_____	_____	_____	_____

	Rarely	Never	Often	Sometimes
26. Future Career	_____	_____	_____	_____
27. Acceptance from Peers	_____	_____	_____	_____
28. Avoiding Trouble In School	_____	_____	_____	_____
29. Fighting With Peers	_____	_____	_____	_____
30. Pressure To Use Drugs	_____	_____	_____	_____
31. Creating Problems Embarrassing To Family	_____	_____	_____	_____
32. Health Issues	_____	_____	_____	_____
33. Setting Goals For Your Future	_____	_____	_____	_____
34. Committing A Criminal Offense	_____	_____	_____	_____
35. Immediate Vs Deferred Gratification	_____	_____	_____	_____

Peer pressure can take away your power to say no; know one has the right to force you into activities that will not result in pro-social positive results.

ADOLESCENT ISSUES
SUMMARY

A. Which of the issues listed have you been experiencing the greatest amount of stress or anxiety from? Write down the number in their order or importance. Do Not Select More Than Six (6).

1. _____   4. _____

2. _____   5. _____

3. _____   6. _____

B. Which of these do you consider urgent to deal with in consultation to improve your understanding and/or behavior

1. _____   3. _____

2. _____   4. _____

C. What areas of concern that are not indicated in items 1 – 35 do you think about at least weekly and consider to be just as important? Describe briefly.

1. _____

   _____

2. _____

   _____

3. _____

   _____

SELF AND OTHER DIRECTED PROGRESS
OF ADOLESCENT
(Another Approach for Assessing)

To what extent do you have the following; each can be assessed 1 thru 10 with ten being the highest positive. Give a brief explanation.

1. Health: Rating _____   Initial _____

_____

_____

_____

_____

2. Feeling of Acceptance: Rating _____   Initial _____

_____

_____

_____

_____

3. Sense of Belonging: Rating _____   Initial _____

_____

_____

_____

_____

4. Harmony With Others: Rating _____   Initial _____

_____

_____

_____

_____

5. Achievement: Rating _____   Initial _____

_____

_____

_____

_____

6. Confidence: Rating _____   Initial _____

_____
_____
_____
_____

7. Understanding: Rating _____   Initial _____
   Society's Expectations

_____
_____
_____
_____

8. Value For Human: Rating _____   Initial _____
   Life

_____
_____
_____
_____

9. Work Ethic: Rating _____   Initial _____

_____
_____
_____
_____

10. Acceptance of Discipline: Rating _____   Initial _____
    From Others

_____
_____
_____
_____

TYPICAL TEACHER OBSERVATIONS OF STUDENTS

	Rarely	Never	Other	Sometimes	Always
1. Good Attendance	____	____	____	_____	____
2. Completes Assignments	____	____	____	_____	____
3. Responds Well To Instructional Questions	____	____	____	_____	____
4. Aggressive Toward Peers	____	____	____	_____	____
5. Well received by Peers	____	____	____	_____	____
6. Learning Retained Well	____	____	____	_____	____
7. Leadership Display	____	____	____	_____	____
8. Generally Happy	____	____	____	_____	____
9. Follows Classroom Procedures	____	____	____	_____	____
10. Provokes Students	____	____	____	_____	____
11. Motivated Toward Academics	____	____	____	_____	____
12. Shows Initiative	____	____	____	_____	____

_____   _____   _____
Student Name (Print)   Grade   Teacher Signature

Partially adapted, with author's personal experience, Howard University, Urban Research Review Vol. 12, November 1, 1989.

2004 STUDENT RESPONSES FROM A DETROIT MIDDLE SCHOOL TO THE QUESTION "WHY SHOULD STUDENTS MAKE EVERY EFFORT TO EXCEL EDUCATIONALLY?"

As a substitute for fifty minutes for an absent co-worker of Social Studies students I surveyed her 7th grade class with the above question. Their responses follow below. All respondents made inspiring ideal/value statements but one in particular which I will begin with had the I need mandate for self.

- I need an Education.
- I want to go to college.
- I want a good job.
- I want to be smart.
- I want to know math.
- I need a good house.
- I need to be a good example.
- I need to have a good reputation around here.
- So you can be successful.
- So you have knowledge.
- So you can be smart and intelligent.
- So you can make a difference.
- So you can show people that black children are smart just like white ones.
- Learn all you can while you can.
- So you can be a good example.
- So you could achieve.
- So you could prove a point.
- Because it took a long time for us to get where we are.
- Hundreds and thousands of black slaves died just so we can walk around Free. We can walk around.
- So I can reach my goal.
- Just to prove the world wrong and make the choice to make it.
- Skeptics say that only 10% percent of us black students today will make it.
- To know how to read, write and count.

Students' Responses to Reasons For Excelling Educationally   **121**

- So I can pass the 12th grade and go on to college.
- So I can reach my goal and pass eighth grade.
- You should excel because you are supposed to.
- To stay out of trouble.
- So one won't be illiterate.
- So the white man can't cheat you.
- You will need what you have been taught to give service in life.
- So I can reach my ultimate plan and goal.
- Make it to higher grade.
- So my family and friends can be proud of me.
- So I can be proud of myself.
- To be smart.
- Colleges may not be accepting blacks if they can't pass the test without affirmative action.
- You'll need to get a job when you get older.
- You can teach family things you already know.
- If you don't know anything you won't become anything.
- I need to know math, science, language arts, social studies and other skills.

TEN ACTION SIGNALS

A review of Awaken the Giant Within by Anthony Robbins has given me further insight on notification of "action signals" that when acknowledged and reflected upon identifies messages to us. How have you been getting your messages most of the time adolescent or what has been communicated to you honorable parents? Robbins asserts that the following primary emotions most people try to avoid but instead should use to drive themselves to action thus over coming problems.

Develop An Action Plan For The Ten Action Signals

1. Discomfort
2. Fear
3. Hurt
4. Anger
5. Frustration
6. Disappointment
7. Guilt
8. Inadequacy
9. Overload/Overwhelmed
10. Loneliness

Source Adapted: Awaken the Giant Within, Robbins, Anthony, Free Press, 1991, pg. 255 - 263

ANALYZE, ASSESS AND DETERMINE ACTION STEPS

I. How have you dealt with this or other problem before? What was the effect?

II. What made it work or not work?

III. How have you tried to resolve this issue?

IV. Are you processing new information?

V. What kinds of things have you done to improve this situation?

VI. What have you done that has made the problem better? Worse? Kept it the same?

VII. What have others done to help you with this; trusted peers, parents or family or other trusted adults? Identify sources.

VIII. What can I learn from this situation to move my life forward?

IX. What have I uncovered about my feelings and convictions?

X. Have I cultivated an attitude of positive expectancy about what will happen in the future?

Partially adapted with authors own experience; source, Interview Strategies for Helpers, W. Cormier and L. Cormier, 2nd Edition, Brooks/Cole Publishing, 1985, pg 214.

WHAT DO I VALUE IN LIFE?

Review the list of values below and rate each item according to the following code:

3   I would sacrifice almost anything else to achieve this.
2   I would work extremely hard to achieve this.
1   I would work hard to achieve this, if it does not interfere too much with
     other values.
0   I do not feel this is of great importance to me.
-   I generally reject this value.

____ Altruism: Having concern for the well-being
      or interests of other people.
____ Power: Possession or control, authority or
      influence over others.
____ Health: The condition of being sound in
      body; freedom from physical disease or
      pain, general well-being.
____ Skill: The ability to do something well as a
      result of training, practice or experience.
____ Justice: The quality of being impartial or
      fair; valuing truth, fact, or reason; having the
      desire to treat others fairly.
____ Emotional well-being: Freedom from over-
      whelming anxieties, tension and inner
      conflict; peace of mind; inner security.
____ Wisdom: The possession of knowledge,
      good sense and good judgment.
____ Pleasure: The feeling of being pleased;
      delight; joy; satisfaction, contentment.
____ Love: A strong feeling of affection and
      fondness; warm attachment, enthusiasm,
      on devotion.
____ Religious Faith: Having a belief in God
      and practicing some form of religion.
____ Honesty: Fairness or straightforwardness
      of conduct; sincerity; truthfulness, frankness.

____ Aesthetics: The appreciation and
      enjoyment of beauty for beauty's sake.
____ Wealth: Large amounts of valuable
      Material possessions, property,
      money or riches.
____ Physical appearance: Concern for the
      beauty of one's own body.
____ Morality: The believe in and keeping
      of Ethical and moral standards.
____ Knowledge: The seeking of truth,
      information, or principles for the
      satisfaction of curiosity, for use, or for
      the power of knowing.
____ Recognition: Being made to feel
      significant and important; being
      given special notice or attention.
____ Achievement: Accomplishment; a
      result brought about by one's effort
      and persistence. "To attain a desired
      end or aim."
____ Autonomy: The ability to be inde-
      pendent and not controlled by others.
____ Loyalty: Maintaining faithfulness
      to a Person, group, institution or
      political system.

Now assume that you have 100 points that can be distributed in any way you please among the values which you have coded with one or more pluses. Divide your 100 points in such a way that they represent the relative importance you attach to each of the plus-coded values. Record or write points at the end of each value word sentence you choose in parenthesis, such as, (30) at the end of Power sentence following others . (30) then spread and divide remaining (70) points as you please following the value word sentences you choose.

Strategies for Understanding and Enriching Today's Youth

OBSTACLES TO SUCCESS CAUSE US TO STRETCH

Congratulations, by now our adolescents, if not before, are hopefully soaring with energy towards their dreams with determined forethought that they deserve the ultimate "pay off." Many peaks and valleys have culminated and your stamina for focusing long range has been trying but you still have the potential for greatness. Your classmates have rendered many fine quotes in your Year Book validating your aims and proven ability and that you have what it takes. This scenario is a tribute to any youngster and his/her significant others.

We are reminded as I am reminded looking at decade old notes from an inspiring/dynamic/motivational WTVS Les Brown presentation that there will be obstacles some of which are:

- Fears; some of these fears will be emotional fear of failing but stretch; also other fears will surface including fear of success, in other words "Will I Be Ready For The Responsibility?" I have heard fear referred to as False Evidence Appearing Real.

- Becoming satisfied; attaining the interim goals can bring on a comfort zone whereas continuing on would yield no discernible difference in rewards; not so, we should like the state of continually prevailing. We must stretch.

- Not feeling worthy; there is nothing wrong with having self-esteem abundance; you have decided your purpose; be obedient to your self,

- help others, and nurture your truth about you and your mentors. Avoid procrastination and squandering time.

- Complaining and blaming everybody; we are responsible for our happiness with less blaming and complaining. We are to determine what we want and that we deserve it. We must stretch and problem solve as the need dictates.

- Circumstances; I am doing what I am supposed to be doing; If circumstances change as an opportunity to a temporary pause stay prepared and empowered. Make a commitment to be happy for the moment thus giving your self a chance to transcend circumstances.

Powerful Motivational Les Brown Quotes To Which I Can Attest:

- "You must be positive even when things are not going your way"

- "Don't burn your bridges behind"

- "When you decide to go to another level all hell breaks out!"

- "Unless you change your behavior your going to produce the same results"

- "If you cannot become your best you cannot be happy"

- "The greatest joy in life is working with young people"

IN CLOSING:
A REVISITATION COMMITMENT

A resounding message I have heard throughout childhood and adulthood is that the faith and works experience builds Christian character. I have received inspiration as I am sure other parents have from knowing our fore-fathers and mothers accepted responsibility for what they would become given the options of opportunities. Access to opportunity required different strategy modes; slave insurrections, escapes, abolitionist movements (white and black), law enactments, civil rights protest and individual perseverance to succeed. We are still capable of enlightening our children with formidable beliefs to over-come and win.

As we parents revisit our aims and goals we remind ourselves that we must continue to take responsibility for what we will become thus becoming role models. Our forefathers and mothers had to have undaunted courage to under-go slavery and subsequently overcome Southern Black Codes and Jim Crow laws. In helping our youth/children interpret reality and life experiences parti-cularly as adolescents to answer "Who Have I Become?" and "Who Will I Become?" we are building a strong Foundation. Evolving from this comes truth and confidence to "press on. "

As our students espouse herein their reasons for excelling we, with love, re-dedicate ourselves to their Fundamental needs and to their dreams and aspirations. We will surely, win with the omnipotent power of the creator God if we don't quit. One of my many happy moments parenting, follows pic-torially.

Let us hold fast our hope without wavering; (For He is faithful that promised;) Hebrews 10:23

Strategies for Understanding and Enriching Today's Youth

GLOSSARY

Acculturation   The process of blending in and taking on characteristics of value from another culture.

Adapting   Recognizing the aims and goals of a social structure while learning appropriate responses in relationships with others thus resulting in helpful growth and self expression (adolescent examples; attends basketball practice timely and consistently, follows instructions of coach, receives validation and gives positive validation both of which affect teamwork and trust, and demonstrates assertiveness confidence in competitive situations).

Adolescence   Means for Latin word adolescere "To Grow Up" or "Grow Into Maturity." Not a sharply defined age span it is the period of sexual, social, ideological and vocational adjustment, and of striving for independence from parents. The criterion for termination of adolescence is linked to the degree to which these adjustments are made.

Amalgamation   Process whereby social distinctions disappear through marriage and reproduction.

Amendment 13th: 1865, Ratified December 18, abolished slavery

Amendment 14th: 1868, Guarantees all citizens the same legal right

Amendment 15th: 1870, Gives all male citizens the right to vote, regardless of race.

Anomie	When norms cease to be effective at controlling peoples behavior; a state of "normlessness" is present.
Assimilation	Gradual loss of distinctiveness of minority groups absorbed into dominant population.
Authoritarian Parenting	Parent attempts to shape, control and evaluate the behavior and attitudes of the child in accordance with absolute standards, valuing obedience for preservation of traditional structure.
Authoritative Parenting	Parent attempts to direct the child's activities but in rational, issue-oriented manner. Verbal give and take is valued and the reasoning behind the decision is shared with child. Parent does not regard self as infallible.
Beliefs	Conceptions or ideas about the world and human Life that center on the meaning of the human experience.
Black Codes	With emancipation January 1, 1863, many states sought to impose restrictions on blacks to prevent them from having equal social status with whites; confederate states developed Black Codes some of which follow. Mississippi was the first to enact these laws in November 1865.

- ❖ No votes and could not serve on juries
- ❖ Denied commonly practiced right to bear arms
- ❖ Right to own land restricted
- ❖ Prohibited from intruding unasked among whites
- ❖ Any white man could arrest a Negro
- ❖ Severe vagrancy laws were passed; i.e., Freedman looking for family members.
- ❖ Negro workers were known as "servants" and employers as "masters."
- ❖ Masters could whip workers under 18 years of age and older workers by judicial order.

❖ Young blacks under the age of eighteen could be apprenticed to their former owners. If they were orphaned or if it were determined that their parents did not have the ability to support them.

❖ Employers through affidavit could before the justice of the peace or police board member could issue a warrant against a legally employed Negro considered a deserter from work or absent from work.

Freedmen Bureau   Vast relief organization created in March 1865, to take care of the immediate economic needs of the freed slaves (food, clothing, shelter, medical care, jobs, and legal help to both blacks and whites). Also to meet educational needs over 4,600 schools were set up for newly freed people.

Civil Rights Act of 1866   Designed to protect the Freedmen from the Black Codes and other repressive legislation. The measure conferred citizenship on Negroes and set the stage for the Fourteenth Amendment.

Colonialism   Political domination of a weak nation by a more Powerful nation.

Comte, Auguste   (1798 – 1857) Person most frequently identified as the so-called Founder of Sociology. Comte proposed a positive philosophy in the study of society.

Conflict Model Of Society   Society viewed as coercive system; recognition of values in shaping institutions but ever-present conflict between those interest that seek to maintain and have them treated as moral entities and those interest that seek to deinstitutionize power.

Contraculture   The idea of opposition to or conflict with the norms and values of the dominant culture.

Jim Crow Laws   Separation of white and black people with equal connotation i.e., separate public transportation seating, drinking fountains, etc. Jim Crow laws were mainly enacted as the union military left in 1877, when reconstruction ended and there after into the 20th Century

Culture

A complex set of learned and shared beliefs, customs, skill, habits, traditions and knowledge common to the members of society. It is learned through socialization.

Dependant Variable

A variable measured by a researcher that follows in time, and changes as a result of changes in, one or more independent variables (Cause and effect relationship).

Dual Consciousness

Recognition of self worth and achievements while simultaneously recognizing ideas and actions that the dominant group perpetuates in an attempt to halt, exclude or neutralize legitimate minority self and/or group efforts to advance.

W.E.B. Dubois

(1868 – 1963) He advocated that African American fight for their rights to vote and was out spoken about racial injustice.

➢ Educator / Wilberforce University 1894
➢ Writer
➢ Social Scientist

First African American to achieve the honor of earning a doctorate degree from Harvard University in 1895. Helped to Found NAACP National Association for the Advancement of Colored People in 1909. He wrote nineteen books and numerous articles including the Souls of Black Folks. He received his First Bachelor's degree from Fisk University in 1888. After dual consciousness rooted in contemporary thought of American thinkers thought such as Emerson and Johnson he would assert for blacks as an American, a Negro, two ideals apart, as treatment and ideals remain unrecognized.

Ego	Primary task is that of adapting to the environment per Freud; through perception, memory and judgement one arrives at an accurate understanding of self, of others and the physical environment.
Erik H. Erikson	(1902 – 1994) A giant in psychology; recipient of Pulitzer Prize and award for biography of Gandhi is Truth both won in 1970.

> Gifted observer and classifier of human behavior and experience
> Understood outstandingly well the emergent phenomena in human growth
> Came to United States in 1933 from Frankfort and Main Germany.
> Graduated from the Vienna Psychoanalytic Institute in 1933.
> Practicing psycho analyst 1933 – 94.
> Teacher and researcher of human development

Authored at least sixteen or more books. He brought new feelings and attitudes within the continuous pattern of the human life cycle. Many biography contributors and colleagues consider him the most widely known psychoanalyst.

Sigmund Freud (1856 – 1939) Viennese Physician and Founder of Psychoanalysis who theorized:

> Sex drive all appears soon after birth biological factors are basic in Freud's theory.
> Psychosexual theory: Three stages the oral, anal, and the phallic introduced concept of fixation and regression. Erotic sensations are continuous and irresistible.
> Personality develops from the inside. Oedipus Complex.

Groups	Small numbers of people joined together in intimate relationships by common interests, values or emotions identifications having group building functions and at times non-functional patterns of behavior.
Hypothesis	A prediction about the relationship about the relationship between two or more variables.
Id	Strives to maximize pleasure and minimize pain, per Freud most mature personality have this infantile core. One of Freud's personality structure which drives hunger, thirst and sex functions. Primitive in content.
Independent Variable	A variable that may be manipulated by a researcher and that precedes in time and produces changes in a dependent variable.
Institutions	Values, norms and beliefs about certain areas of human activity, such as economics, religion or education.
Integration Model Society	A complex whole of interrelated parts which assumes That dominant value patterns shape human behavior; Shared values are treated as "Moral Entities." Stability is more valued than change.
Learning Theorist	Socio-psychologist who generally regard personality as developing from the "Outside In"; parental standards and societal prescriptions are learned by reinforcement and imitation, and are adopted as the child's own.
Norms	Expected behavior in given situations.
Multi-cultural Diversity	Ethnicities sharing common ideas and beliefs in a pluralistic society can retain their identity and yet participate in American cultural themes.

Peer Group	A group formal or informal with common frames of reference or (common bond) to carryout specific functions and activities and/or to satisfy expedient needs; further as an important reference, peer groups can shape youth's personal values, their goals, aspirations and sense of belonging.
Role	Describes the behavior of one who occupies the status.
Self	Person's conception of what and who he/she is slowly emerges from his interaction with others having lasting effects on the core of the personality.
Self Actualization	Generating emotions, ideas and actions in a responsible way and in a direction which will enable one to confirm his/her self worth while progressively achieving goals and making adjustments.
Socialization	A lifelong process. It begins very early, and in due course the child learns to take part in group life by learning the values of the group and society socialization regulates behavior but it allows for individuality and self awareness. The parent as the primary agent imparts skills, knowledge and values and as such are themselves socialized in taking on the parental role.
Social Underclass	A culturally defined group usually functioning below their potential usually delineated by societal social/educational/economic strata and whose choices and outcomes have been hampered by inaccessibility to opportunity, missed opportunities and/or under developed preparation to meet free enterprise demands but yet unrelenting toward achievement.

Society   Defined as a number of people who have been together long enough to become organized to some degree and who share a common culture.

Sociology   Basic aim is to discover the basic structure of human society, to identify the main forces that hold groups together or weaken them and to learn the conditions that transform social life. Sociology illuminates aspects of social life through observation, hypothesizing and testing that otherwise might be obscurely recognized.

Statuses   Either achieved or ascribed are ranked in value or prestige; a position in society is defined as status.

Superego   Contains per Freud moral precepts and ideas; punishes the individual with guilt when he transgresses; can be as primitive as Id.

Values   Goals and standards in which people have great emotional investment; abstract standards that exist over time and identify what is right and proper in a society.

SUGGESTED READING

Berns, Roberta., Child, Family, Community: Holt, Rinehart, Winston, Inc., 1974.

Besger, Peter L., and Thomas Luckman, The Social Construction of Reality (GardenCity, N.Y. : Doubleday and Company 1966).

Billings, Gloria Ladson, The Dreamkeepers, San Francisco, Jossey, Bass Publishers, 1994.

Billingsley, Andrew, Black Families In White America, New Jersey: Prentice Hall, Inc., 1968.

Broom, Leonard and Selznick, Philip, Principles of Sociology, New York: Harper and Rowe Publishers, 1970.

Bullock, Henry A., A History of Negro Education in the South, Mass: Harvard Press, 1967.

Coleman, J.S. The Adolescent Society: The Social Life of the Teenager and its Impact on Education. New York: Free Press, 1961.

Comer, James P. and Poussaint, Alvin F., Psychiatrist, Raising Black children, New York: Penguin Group, 1992.

Cormier, Wm., and Cormier, L. Sherilyn, Interviewers Strategies for Helpers, California: Brooks/Cole Pulishing Co., 1985.

Crandall, J. Achievement. In H.W. Stevenson (Ed.) Child Psychology. 62 Yearbook, National Study for the Study of Education. Chicago: University of Chicago Press, 1963.

Crandell, V. S., Katkowsky, W., and Crandell, V. J., Children's Beliefs in Their Own Control of Reinforcements in Intellectual-Academic Achievement Situations, Child Development, 1965, 36, 91-109.

Du Bois, W.E.B., The Cultural Mission of Atlanta University, Phylon, 3 (1942), reprinted, Meyer, Weinberg, ed., W.E.B. Bois, New York: Harper and Row, 1970.

Du Bois, W.E.B., The World and Africa, p. 155

Eichhorn, Donald H., The Middle School, New York: The Center for Applied Research in Education, Inc., 1966.

Erickson, Erik, Childhood and Society, 2nd ed., (New York: W.W. Norton and Company 1963.

Erickson, Erik, Identity and the Life Cycle, Psychological Issues, Monograph1, Vol. 1, No. 1, New York: International Universities Press, 1959.

Erickson, Erik, Identity and the Life Cycle, A Re-issue, Norton, 1980.

Feldman, S. Shirley and Glen R. Elliott, eds. At the threshold, The Developing Adolescent, Cambridge, Mass; Harvard University Press, 1990.

Foner, The Life and Writings of Frederick Douglass, Vol III, p. 261.

Foner, The Life and Writings of Frederick Douglass, Penguin Books, 1984.

Foster, William, The Negro People in American History, New York: International Publishers,1970.

Frazier, Franklin, Black Bourgeoise, Principles of Sociology, Harper
    and Rowe Publishers.

Freed, Aaron, Conduct and Conscience: The Socialization of Internalized
    Controlled Behavior, New York: Academic Press, 1968.

Hamby/Knudsey Perucci, Sociology, Basic Structures and Processes.

Henry, William A., Beyond the Melting Pot: Time Magazine, April 9, 1990.

Introduction to Group Dynamics; What It Is? Main ideas, its language and its
    applications: Association Press, 291 Broadway, New York,
    N.Y. 10007, 1966.

Jones, Matthew D., Raising Boys to Become Responsible Men,
    Self Published, 2004.

Kunjufu, Jawanza, "To Be Popular or Smart", "Developing Positive Self
    Images and Discipline in Black Children" and "Countering The
    Conspiracy to Destroy Black Boys", Volumes I, II, III, IV, African
    American Images, Chicago, Illinois.

Landis, Judson R., Sociology: Concepts and Characteristics, 2nd Education,
    Wadsworth Publishing Company.

Myrdal, Gunnar, "An American Dilemma," The Negro Problem and Modern
    Democracy, Vol. II: Harper Torch Books, Harper and Row Publishers,
    New York, 1969.

Mills, C. Wright, The Sociological Imagination, Oxford University Press, 1959.

Mills, C. Wright, The Powers Elite, Oxford University Press, 1956.

Ploski, Harry A. and Williams, James, The Negro Almanac, Fifth Edition,
    Detroit, Detroit/New York: Gale Research, Detroit.

Robbins, Anthony, Awaken The Giant Within, New York: Free Press, 1991.

Rogers, R. Carl, On Becoming a Person; A Therapist View of Psychotherapy, Western Behavioral Sciences Institute La Jolla, California, Houghton Mifflin Company, Boston, 1961.

Sebald, Hans, Adolescence, A Sociological Analysis: Appleton-Century-Crafts, New York, 1968.

Silberman, Charles E., Crisis in Black and White, Vintage Brooks: Division of Random House, 1964.

Wenar, Charles, Personality Development: Houghton Mifflin Company, Boston, 1971.

Williams, George, History of the Negro Race in America 1619 – 1880, New York and London G.P. Putnam's Sons, The Knickerbockers Books Press, 1882.

REFERENCES

1. Andrew Hacker, Two Nations Black and White, Separate, Hostile, Unequal (New York: Ballantine Books, 1992). pg. 68

2. Dr. James B. Comer and Dr. Alvin F. Poussaint, Raising Black Children, (New York: Penguin Books U.S.A. Inc., 1992/Plume Printing, PP 11-12.

3. Charles Wenar, Personality Development from Infancy to Adulthood (Boston: Houghton Mifflin Co., 1971), PP. 26-28.

4. M. Scott Peck, M.D., The Road Less Traveled (New York: Touchbook, Simon and Schuster, 1979), P 126.

5. Wenar, Personality Development, PP. 359-360

6. Ibid, P 360

7. Ibid, P 360

8. Ibid, P 360

9. Ibid, P 362

10. Ibid, P 362

11. Paul George and Gordon Lawrence, Handbook for Middle School Teachers (Scott Foresman and Company, 1982), PP. 43-44

12. Donald Eichhorn, The Middle School (New York: Center for Applied Research in Education, Inc., 1966), P 93.

NOTES

"Every Step is Upward Lifting as We Climb."